Reasoning about the World as the Flow of All

Richard L. "Arf" Epstein

Advanced Reasoning Forum

The moral rights of the author have been asserted.

Names, characters, and incidents relating to any of the characters in this text are used fictitiously, and any resemblance to actual persons, living or dead, is entirely coincidental. *Honi soit qui mal y pense.*

First printing November, 2024.

For more information visit our website:
    www.AdvancedReasoningForum.org
Or contact us:
    Advanced Reasoning Forum
    P. O. Box 635
    Socorro, NM 87801   USA
    rle@AdvancedReasoningForum.org

ISBN 978-1-938421-58-7   print
ISBN 978-1-938421-59-4   e-book

CONTENTS

PREFACE

The WORLD and LANGUAGE
    1   Flux and Continuity 2
    2   The World as the Flow of All 3

CATEGOREMATIC WORDS
    3   Base Categorematic Words and Contexts 8
    4   Concepts 13
    5   Adjectives and Adverbs 15
    6   Categorematic Words as Modifiers 17
    7   Together-Uses of Categorematic Words 21
    8   Linking Categorematic Words 26
    9   Disjoining Categorematic Words 29
    10   Negative Categorematic Words 31
           Summary 34

COMPOUND WORDS
    11   Compound Words 38
    12   Examples 41

FORM and CONTENT
    13   Forms of Words 46
    14   How Words Elicit Concepts and Can Be Used to Describe 51

CONCEPTUAL EQUIVALENCE
    15   Conceptual Equivalence and Descriptive Equivalence 56
    16   Deriving Conceptual Equivalences 61

REASONING
    17   Inferences and Validity 66
    18   Scenarios 69
    19   Examples of Evaluating in Scenarios 73
    20   A System for Deriving Valid Words and Valid Inferences, **IXN** 80

TALK of CONTEXT in the FLOW of ALL
    21   Words for Contexts 88
    22   Examples 93
    23   Forms of Words 99
    24   How Words Can Be Used to Describe 103
    25   Inferences and Validity 104
    26   A System for Reasoning with Words Marked for Context, **WMC** 107
    27   Local Categorematic Words 110

28	Examples: Stability and Change	115
29	Names Replaced by Descriptions?	119
30	A System of Reasoning with Local Words, **WMC+Local**	120

CONCLUDING

31	Different Ways of Encountering the World	122

APPENDICES

A.	Color Words as Process Words or Mass Terms	128
B.	Compound Nouns and Meaning	131
C.	Negation in Mass-Process Languages	134
D.	Strawson on Mass Terms and Individuals	135
E.	Talk of Time in the Flow of All	137
F.	Expanding Our Talk in the Flow of All ?	140

BIBLIOGRAPHY	145
LIST of CONTEXT WORDS	148
INDEX of EXAMPLES	149
INDEX of SYMBOLS	153
INDEX	154

Acknowledgements

So many have helped me learn how to talk and reason in the flow of all. But my memory of who said what is not good. And there are, I am sure, many whom I have forgotten in my old age. But at least I can thank those who come to mind now. Juan Francisco "Pancho" Rizzo, Fred Kroon, William S. "Bill" Robinson, Peter Adams, Ivan da Costa Marques, Eduardo "Eddie" Ribeiro, Kris Hardy, Chad Hansen, Chris Sinha, Alex Raffi, Michael Rooney, Arnold Mazotti, Suely Porto Alves, Melissa Axelrod, Esperanza Buuitrago Diaz, Walter Carnielli, João Marcos—so many, and so many whom I cannot recall, some still with us and others who have passed into the flow of all, the flow of love. My gratitude knows no bounds. May you be blessed with such friends.

November, 2024

Preface

As speakers of English, German, or Romance languages it is hard for us to conceive of the world as flux, the flow of all, with no or only a quite secondary idea of individual things that persist through their changes. In *Language and the World: Essays New and Old* I've tried to make it possible for you to enter that way of encountering the world with essays by linguists and anthropologists who have described people who talk and live with that conception. That is important and useful background, but not essential, for I have set out the basic idea of the world as flow in the first two chapters. In this volume I hope to explore more clearly that conception by asking how we can reason in accord with it.

This is an attempt, a first attempt as far as I know, to give a systematic analysis of how to reason that is not tied to our European languages, to step out of our language conceptions and habits. Consider then this work as a bridge, a chance for us as speakers of languages that focus primarily on the world as made up of things to begin to see the richness and complexity of encountering the world as the flow of all, the one and not many. The contrasts, often unsettling, can lead us to understand better how we encounter and reason about the world as made up of things.

> The world is not digital; the world is analog.
> —Peter Adams

> We do not live in the world. We make a world in which we live.
> —Arf

> A wink is as good as a nod to a blind man.
> —traditional

> It's like trying to change bicycles in the middle of a river.
> —anonymous

CAST of CHARACTERS

Ralph

Bon Bon (L) and Chocolate (R)

Bidú (L) and Arf (R)

Chocolate (L) and Birta (R)

Arfito

chickens, sheep, and Bon Bon in the corral
— see page 8 of the text —

Birta, Chocolate, and Bidú, and the chickens have now
passed into the flow of all, the flow of love.

Dogshine

corral and shed

though
The World and Language

1 Flux and Continuity

We have two great certainties in our lives. We are certain that all changes, that nothing stays the same, that all is flux. This is our first experience of the world, our earliest perception. And later we have the certainty that some things persist, some things are the same. The ball we played with yesterday is the same we have in our hand today, this house is the same house. The certainty that things persist in time is overlaid on our certainty that all is flux, for we believe in the continuity of the ball, the house, though we know that they are not the same: the ball has been scuffed, the house has been painted. Our certainty that things persist is contradicted by our understanding that all is flux, but we hold to it nonetheless. We construct our certainty in the persistence of things from our experience of the flux, learning quite young how to establish correlations, equivalences, sameness of things. This is the same ball, the same house, where we learn that what we mean by "same" depends on the kind of thing.

Nowhere is this more evident than in our certainties about ourselves. Nothing is more certain to us than that we change: we cut a finger, we get a haircut, we cannot see as well as we once did, we have a backache, we limp, we squint when we could see so well before. And we believe differently now: we see our first love so differently, we remember and understand the job we left, the friends we still have from former times in a very different way, all summed up in "If I knew then what I know now ...". We know we change, but our greatest certainty, beyond the certainty that we change, beyond the certainty that all is flux, beyond the certainty that things persist, is that there is an "I", a me, a single person that persists, that unifies the changes in our physique and the changes in our perceptions. This "I" we are certain of from the time we first become able to formulate the idea when we are very young until we lose the ability to formulate the idea when we are very old.

There is, or sadly I should say was Juney. She was a black and white border collie. The first day I met her my neighbor, an elderly lady, had just got her from a relative who didn't want the dog and who had kept Juney tied up. My neighbor asked me to tie Juney in my yard while she had some relatives over because Juney was too active, a young dog, almost a puppy, and wild. I tied her up in my yard and went to pet her. She bit at me, afraid, unhappy to be tied up again. That was Juney on that day. And the Juney of each day thereafter, slowly learning to trust me, going for a walk with me every day. And the Juney of two years later, who would pass up her food to go for a walk with me, who would not go into my neighbor's home at night but would lie outside my kitchen window looking up at me. There was one Juney, I say, knowing that there was a unity, a single Juney, that somehow, some way, unifies each of those daily Juneys. The closest we can come to recognizing in our talk both our certainty of the unity and our certainty of the flux is to use a single name, "Juney".

2 The World as the Flow of All

The world is made up of things: rocks, tables, dogs, people, stars. Of this we are sure, for we have words for all these and many more.

We know of process and change, too. For example, suppose I show you an apple. It's round, red, shiny. I take a bite of it. It's changed—no longer round, no longer red and shiny where I bit into it. I take another bite. The apple has changed some more. I take another bite, and another, and the apple has changed a lot. I give the core to my donkey. The apple is all gone.

The apple changed. But is that the apple I started with? If one apple changed, it wasn't what I first showed you, it wasn't what I bit into the second time, it wasn't the core. It must have been something beyond all those, somehow beyond any particular time, something that persists through all "its" changes. Talking of change we find ourselves talking about things beyond any particular time.

Change, we feel, is not real like things are real, like rocks, tables, dogs, people, the sun. The sun? Everything we know about that fiery ball tells us that the sun is a process: nothing endures in it, not shape, not form, not even molecules—only the process. A rock, too, is process, changing, never stable, though we don't notice the changes. The difference isn't that the sun is a process and the rock is a thing; the difference is the scale of time over which we note "changes".

Our focus in our language is on the world as made up of things, on stability in the flow of our experience. Still, we have some sense in our lives of flow, of flux, of change, of process. And we have some hints of that in our language.

Suppose you're in my living room with me, and I look out the window and say,

It's raining.

Yes, that's true. But what's raining? There's no "it": the weather isn't raining. The weather is rainy; the weather doesn't do anything. The word "it" is a dummy, there because in English every verb requires a subject. I could have said just

Raining.

You would have understood me. It's clear I'm talking about now, which is all the "is" in the original sentence tells us. And it's clear I'm talking about there, outside the window, though in English we don't require any word or phrase to mark that.

On a winter day I might point and say "Snowing", and you'd understand me. That's complete, clearly true or false, though it doesn't look like a sentence in English. Or I could say, "Sun-ing" or "Breeze-ing", which are odd, but once you've got the hang of my talking this way, you'd understand me.

If we were at my friend's apartment in the city, I might look out the window and say,

Running.

You'd understand me. It sounds odd because I haven't said who or what is running. That seems essential when we talk English because verbs are descriptions of what's happening to or because of a thing. Yet running is running, whether it's one person, a dog chasing a cat, or lots of people in a marathon. I don't describe all when I say "Running", but we never describe all. What I've said is true or false, enough to communicate.

Looking out my window at the patio at home I could say "Barking" and you'd understand me. On another day looking at my dogs I could say, "Sleeping". These are process words, and used this way they begin to become part of a way to describe process without a focus on things.

After a rain, as I look out at the patio I might say "Mud". Mud isn't a thing. We don't say "There are three muds out there." We say "There's some mud", because mud is a mass. Water, gold, snow are masses, too. We know they're some of the world, different from things. Every part of mud is mud, while no part of an apple is an apple. Processes are like that, too. Every part of raining is raining, and there's no smallest part of raining, for a single drop of water is not raining.

Starting to see the world as process-mass, I look out the window and say, "Dog-ing". You'd understand, though it seems incomplete. One dog or many dogs? What's the dog doing? We need a verb and an indication of singular or plural when we talk in English. Yet if I say, "There's a dog", the verb is just "is". The dog is there, it exists there, that's all. "Dog-ing", understood as about there and now, does that as well, though it doesn't say whether there's one or many, whether alive or dead, whether big or small. Much is left out, but much is left out of our description "There's a dog."

I could turn, and looking around the room say, "Table-ing". You'd understand. An odd way to talk, but true. Or pointing to the next room I could say, "Woman-ing". Odd too, incomplete, but true. We are beginning to see the world as made up of processes.

Processes? To say that is to slip back into thing-talk. This process, that process, one process, two processes, a fast process, a blue process. No. To see process in the world there are not processes, just process. The world is flux. Words like "raining", "sun-ing", "running", "dog-ing", "mud-ing" describe the flow of all in some context. They don't pick out separate parts of the flow any more than "Pacific Ocean" and "Baltic Sea" pick out parts separate and distinct from the water that covers the earth.

To talk of the world as the flow of all we can borrow and modify some words from English like "raining", "running", "dog-ing", "mud-ing", "woman-ing". We add "-ing" to remind us of our new way of talking, of seeing. When we specify a context, we have a "sentence" that is true or false. Pointing out the window now, if I say "Cat-ing", that's false. And just as "Raining" is true or false, "Woman-ing" is true or false, and "Mud-ing" is true or false.

I could point to my patio and say "Brown-ing" and that would be true, for my old brown dog Birta is there. We can use "Brown-ing" as much as "Dog-ing" to describe in the flow of all. There is no distinction between what we call adverbs and adjectives because there are no nouns and no verbs, no words for things and what is done by or to them. There are only words meant to describe in the flow of all.

This seems far from how we understand the world as made up of things, more like a vision that a mystic might try to convey. Yet it is the basis of many spoken languages, such as Navajo and Chinese.

In this book I will show how we can develop ways to talk and reason about the world as the flow of all, describing but not partitioning. In doing so we will come to a better understanding of this way of being in the world and also a better understanding of how our own language directs us to experience the world as made up of things. These ways will not be the whole story of talking and reasoning about the world as the flow of all but a guide to help us grasp the basic outlines. We will find that the understanding of the world as the flow of all is not mysticism but a change of grammar.

In *Language and the World: Essays New and Old* I and others investigate this different way of encountering the world and show how it leads to differences in how we live. That book is important not only as motivation for developing ways for reasoning about the world as the flow of all but also as a guide for how to think of the world as the flow of all. Here it is enough that you have some idea of what will be the basis of our work on how to talk and reason about the world as the flow of all.

the world as the flow of all

the world as made up of things

Categorematic Words

3 Base Categorematic Words and Contexts

Every language has base words, roots, or stems that carry the concepts the speakers of the language use in communicating. They are the *categorematic* parts of speech. They, or rather we using them, establish the categories of the language culture. They can stand alone, as in Chinese. Or they can be placed in speech only with modifications, with prefixes, suffixes, infixes, as in Salishan languages.[1]

In our work here, I'll assume we have such concept words. Some will be grammatically indivisible, the base words, that can stand alone to make an assertion, as when pointing to my old dog Birta I say "dog". In order to have examples for our discussions, I'll coin some from English.

DOG-ing	MUD-ing	SNOW-ing
BARK-ing	SKUNK-ing	SMOKE-ing
RUN-ing	UNICORN-ing	HATE-ing
CAT-ing	RAIN-ing	LOVE-ing
MEOW-ing	BANANA-ing	FLOWER-ing
SUN-ing	WIND-ing	ELEPHANT-ing
RUTABAGA-ing	JUSTICE-ing	GRAPE-ing

I use all capital letters to remind us that these are not meant to be of any grammatical part of speech of English. And I add "-ing" to relate them to English gerunds that are half noun-half verb, half mass term-half process word, suggesting the movement of the flow of all, though there is nothing to move, nor even to flow, but just all. They are waiting for a grammar to show how they will be used, not as nouns or verbs or adjectives but as evoking concepts for describing but not partitioning.

In this list we have words that we as English speakers would consider to stand for masses: "MUD-ing", "SNOW-ing". We have words that we as English speakers would consider to stand for processes: "RUN-ing", "HATE-ing". We have words that we as English speakers would consider to pick out things: "BANANA-ing", "UNICORN-ing". And we have words that we as English speakers have no clear conception of as process, mass, or thing, such as "JUSTICE-ing". It is not that each of these words is a word for a mass or process or even a thing conceived of as a mass or process. We are to think of them as describing in the flow of all, not process, not mass, but simply describing. From our thing-language perspective, "DOG-ing" can be used to describe dog-ing, essence of dog, a dog, dogs, and more.[2]

---

[1] See the essays in *Language and the World*.
[2] This is why I've abandoned calling them "mass-process words" as in my earlier writings.

Categorematic words   *Categorematic words* evoke the concepts of the language that we can use to describe in the flow of all.

A *base categorematic word* is one that is grammatically indivisible.

Categorematic words used to describe in context
Using a base categorematic word, we hope to describe in the flow of all, to direct someone's attention. When I say "RAIN-ing" and point out the window, that utterance is a good/accurate/correct description in that context or it is not. That's because the context indicates that I'm talking about now and outside the window. By itself, "RAIN-ing" is just a way to describe, not a description. Some context, established physically or with other words, is needed to make a base word into a description.

Correct descriptions   A categorematic word used to describe in a context is a good/accurate/correct description or it is not. Briefly, we say that the description is *correct* or *incorrect* in context.

An *assertion* is an utterance or inscription of a word in context meant to be judged as correct or incorrect.

In saying "RAIN-ing" while pointing out the window, when that's correct I do not direct someone's attention to a part of the flow of all. That would be to take parts of the flow of all as things, yet raining is not a part of the flow of all. There is only my pointing to establish context, and I have used correctly the way of describing in the context with "RAIN-ing". There is no suggestion that "RAIN-ing" describes all in the context, for "DOG-ing", "MUD-ing", and other categorematic words are also correct to assert when I point out the window.

A context can be established in many ways. For example:

"RAIN-ing"	pointing	is correct or incorrect
"DOG-ing"	touching a cat	is correct or incorrect
"SMOKE-ing"	smelling	is correct or incorrect
"WIND-ing"	feeling the breeze	is correct or incorrect
"GRAPE-ing"	tasting a spoonful of jam	is correct or incorrect
"SHEEP-ing"	saying "At the corral last week"	is correct or incorrect
"RUN-ing"	saying "after BARK-ing and before SLEEP-ing"	is correct or incorrect

It is tempting to say that a context is a possibility. But that seems odd to say about these examples. Rather, establishing a context is like picking out a possibility. But that, too, seems odd, for what is the possibility when smelling? The notion of a categorematic word being correct relative to a context seems much more physical and behavioral than any idea we have of possibility. Establishing a context is nothing more, and nothing less, than getting someone, perhaps oneself, to pay attention with us.

We establish a context; we don't recognize a context, for a context is not a thing. When I get you to smell, that's not a thing. Yet in what follows, I'll talk of all contexts in which, say, "ELEPHANT-ing" could be correct to assert, which seems to depend on thinking of contexts as things. I'll talk of some context in which "HATE-ing" could be correct, which suggests I'm talking of contexts as things. But that needn't be, any more than when I talk of all mud I am intending for you to think of "muds" as things, or when I talk of some running I am intending for you to think of "runnings" as things.

So in what follows I'll talk of a context, of some context, or of all contexts in which a categorematic word used to describe is correct or could be correct. And speaking English to you, I'll often describe a context using thing-talk. When I talk of pointing as establishing context, I mean that to cover all the ways above as well as pictures, as on p. 8 above.

The suffix "-ing" is useful for reminding us of our new way of using words, but it is distracting. I'll use it now only when I want to emphasize the difference of our language from English. You'll remember, I hope, that "RUN" is not meant to be read as a verb, and "DOG" is not meant to be read as a noun or vice-versa.

Describing what?
Directing our attention we recognize (or not) that a word is a good/accurate/correct description. A description of what? Just a description. What am I describing with "SMELL" in context of my sniffing? I describe smell-ing, and that's all there is to say. What am I describing with "SWEET" in context of you and I tasting some strawberry jam? I describe sweet-ing, and that's all there is to say. We agree or we do not agree that the assertion is correct. Any explanation I could give for what it means for a categorematic word to be correct in a context would not clarify but only obscure.

We touch, we smell, we taste, we hear, we see in the world as the flow of all. We do not assume there is some substance in the world that grounds those. We just touch, smell, taste, hear, see. There is the flow of all which we describe but do not partition.

Focusing on just dog-ing
We have the convention if not illusion that using our thing-language we can focus on just a dog. But we do not have a dog independent of all else even in

our conceiving. The dog is brown or black, sitting or standing, wagging her tail or sleeping.

Some philosophers say we can focus on the dog simpliciter, that thing independent of its properties. Others say this cannot be: any particular dog cannot be disentangled from its properties, whether those be essential or accidental of a particular time. The idea that we can focus our attention on just one thing depends on our distinguishing between things and properties of things. But "DOG", "WAG", "BROWN", "SIT", "BREATHE", are all categorematic words, all play the same role in our talk in the flow of all. There is no difference between mass, process, quality, or property. There is only the flow of all described in different ways.

We do not have contexts in which only "DOG" is correct. We can focus on, pay attention to just dog-ing by using "DOG". That, we indicate, is what we're concerned with in this context, not because it is the only description that is correct in the context.

Names
Names in English are quintessential words for individual things. Can we use them to describe in the flow of all?

What is Zoe? She is a woman; but that's to talk of her as a thing. She doesn't like to be talked of as a thing. She sees herself as more than that, as something that continues in time, has continuity. Being true to that vision, we treat her name as a base categorematic word.

Thinking of the world as made up of things, we have to figure out what unifies all the life of Zoe. What is it that makes Zoe last year the same as Zoe this year, though not the same but the same thing? Do we talk of an "instance" of Zoe? A "time-slice" of Zoe? So we have the time-slice of Zoe at August 2, 2003. But that's a pretty big time. There's the time-slice of Zoe at 10:22 a.m. August 2, 2003. And "smaller and smaller" time-slices. And that looks very much like taking parts of a mass. Viewing the world as the flow of all, "ZOE" is a word we can use to distinguish in the flux; there is no question of unifying the "parts" of Zoe. We can talk of some Zoe-ing, and that way of talking fits better the idea of time-slices than thing-talk. The idea that Zoe is a thing is quite bizarre, absurd, an idea whose justification is only to use nouns and verbs in English (and other thing-languages). There is a whole there, but not one made up of parts, a unity that we know as much as we know the unity of the water in this lake is not the same as the water in that puddle. So in what follows I will take as base categorematic words English words that we consider to be names.[3]

---

[3] In "On What There Is" Willard van Orman Quine seemed to come to this view of proper names. He said that in classical predicate logic we could replace proper names by predicates. So we could use "pegasizes" rather than "Pegasus". That avoids problems with non-referring names but is not consonant with the foundations of predicate logic in which the roles of names and predicates are meant to be quite distinct. See the discussion in Chapter VIII of my *Predicate Logic*.

Aside: Truth
I do not use of the word "true" here because truth, a central concern of Western philosophy for over 2,000 years, has been used in many ways that may or may not be compatible with encountering the world as the flow of all. Nonetheless, the correct–incorrect dichotomy for describing fits the ways we talk of truth and falsity, as described in my paper "Truth and Reasoning".

Aside: Context for assertions in thing-languages?
Speaking English, we can assert a simple sentence like "Juney is barking" without first establishing a context. That's because the sentence gives the context: it's about Juney now. If we wish to assert "All the dogs are barking" we do need to establish context: what dogs? And if someone asserts "Pegasus is a dog" we ask for some context, since there is no thing called "Pegasus" for it to be about.

What are the conditions for "Arfito is a dog" to be true? Arfito is a dog. There's no simpler way to say it, and explanations are so burdened with assumptions and far from experience as to be useless:

- — Arfito has the property of being a dog.
- — Arfito is in the collection of all dogs.
- — Arfito instantiates the universal "dog".
- — Arfito being a dog.

Aside: Chad Hansen on learning concepts
Chad Hansen in *Language and Logic in Ancient China* contrasts the idea of universals meant to stand behind our learning languages with a mass-process view in Chinese.

> Baby Susie learns to utter "doggie" in the presence of Fido (the family dog—a collie) and the neighbor's German shepherd and a few other occasional mongrels as examples. However, the first time she sees Uncle Harry's Afghan hound, she promptly chirps, "Doggie!" How did she know? We tend to say she has learned to abstract from particular examples—learned abstract thinking. She has abstracted from all the particular dogs she had encountered the features common to all dogs. Seeing that the Afghan hound had these features, even though quite different in other respects, she correctly classifies it as a dog. This classification depends on her having learned an abstract idea.
>
> Baby Mei-Ling, on the other hand, has learned to use the word *kou* 'dog' for that stuff which she encounters at Uncle Jang's. But the story told does not involve any abstracting. Rather one says that she has acquired the ability to distinguish dog-stuff from non-dog-stuff.** The problem of learning for Mei-Ling is how she is able to reidentify the same stuff. But expressing the problem in that way makes us less likely to talk of abstracting properties from different objects.
>
> ** In fact, the puzzle about learning is identical in both stories. Our ability to acquire discriminatory skills adequate to learn a language is what needs to be explained. What is hard for us to acknowledge, given our commonsense commitment to mental abstract ideas, is that the detour through ideas doesn't explain that ability at all. pp. 51–52

4 Concepts

When I say that "DOG" elicits a concept for us to communicate, I am not thinking of a concept as some fixed thing that the word stands for or represents. I intend it as Benson Mates describes in *The Skeptic Way*.

> Suppose now that someone were to ask the Socratic-style question, "What *is* a concept?" A standard answer in Sextus's day would be that a concept is a change of state (*kinesis*) of the intellect (M 8.336a).[4] But a somewhat more informative answer, which can be inferred from the use of the terms in actual practice by Sextus and his opponents, is this: a concept is in effect the meaning of a word or noun phrase. To have a concept of human being (*anthropos*) is to know what a human being is (M 8.87ff.); that is, it is to grasp a sense or meaning that is expressed in Greek by the term *anthropos*. Thus when Sextus raises the question of whether *X* is conceivable, he is in effect questioning the very meaningfulness of utterances containing the corresponding word, insofar as that word is to be used in accord with one or another of the Dogmatists' definitions. . . .
>
> However, if we allow that for Sextus and his opponents concepts are in effect the meaning of words, it must be added that these meanings are not to be treated in the Fregean manner as independently existing ideal entities that may be expressed with varying degrees of accuracy by the words we use. Instead, they are to be thought of more "psychologically." Concepts are said to be "formed" by people on the basis of their individual experiences; consequently, since different people will mean different things by a given word, we can expect to be told that they will have different concepts associated with that word.   pp. 22–23

But if each person has a different concept of "DOG", as each must, how can we communicate? We talk, and while we do we point, we sniff, we touch, we draw each other's attention in one way or another so that we can use the word together. Concepts are not things that we must come to grips with. We establish agreements on how to use a word, which for each of us elicits a concept. Those agreements need not be explicit, nor couched in language. We do not need nor can we approach objectivity, and subjectivity leads only to solipsism. We live together in a world of agreements in action, in a world of intersubjectivity.[5]

Concepts and correct use of words
Do we need to talk of concepts? Can't we rely on evaluations of the use of categorematic words in context as correct or incorrect, hoping that by doing so concepts will come along?

I can point and say "javelina" and you can agree with me or disagree. Or

---

[4] [M = *Against the Mathematicians*]
[5] I talk here of concepts, not meaning, because that is less loaded with a history of analyses in the West. Concepts, just as meanings, are not things, they are not attached to a word; they are developed with the use of a word. Concepts are not static but are some of what we do. Concepts, as meaning, are in our bodies, as I explain in "Language-Thought-Meaning".

perhaps you don't know that word, so there's no agreement or disagreement. You are puzzled. So I describe, explain, try to give you "the" concept of "javelina": it's like a small pig, black with short tusks, lives in the riparian ways of the desert areas of the Southwest of the United States and in Mexico, rooting in the earth. Later you point and say "javelina" and I agree: that's correct. You've got it, I think.

But do you? Certainly you don't understand "javelina" as I do, for my experiences have been different from yours, recalling how one chased my dog Chocolate. We try to come to some agreement on the concept of "javelina" through comparing assertions, trying to reduce it to agreeing on contexts in which it is correct to assert it.

But pointing, conditions for correct use, do not suffice to establish concepts. If a child does not know what "FISH" means, any explanation we give of it will include "WATER". But it is correct to assert "FISH" when pointing to a fried trout on a dinner plate. And in any context in which it is correct to assert "PEGASUS" it is correct to assert "DOG"—vacuously, for there is no context in which it is correct to assert "PEGASUS". But in terms of paying attention in the flow of all, the concept (meant to be) elicited by "PEGASUS" does not depend on or include the concept elicited by "DOG". We understand "PEGASUS" through understanding "HORSE", "WING"," FLY", and more.

In order to evaluate whether a word describes correctly in a context we need to understand the word. We may come to that understanding, a concept, through comparing assertions using the word. But it is the concept that the word elicits for us, whether shared or not, that leads us to say that the word is a good/accurate/correct description in a given context. We can use words to communicate only to the extent that in some way we share our concepts.

Concepts and correct descriptions If a word elicits a concept, then in any context that we note, the concept determines for us whether the word is a correct description.

Aside: Agreements (from my *Propositional Logics*, 1st edition p. 401, 3rd edition p. 403)

> The word 'agreement' is wrong, and 'convention' even more so. . . . Almost all our conventions, agreements, assumptions are implicit, tacit. They needn't be either conscious or voluntary. Many of them may be due to physiological, psychological, or, perhaps, metaphysical reasons: for the most part we seem not to know. Agreements are manifested in lack of disagreement and the fact that people communicate. To be able to see that we have made (or been forced into, or simply have) a tacit agreement is to be challenged on it.

Aside: How Helen Keller learned words
Helen Keller was stricken at age nineteen months by a disease that left her deaf and blind. In Chapter 4 of her book *The Story of My Life* she relates how she was finally able to connect the spelling W-A-T-E-R on her hand by her teacher in many contexts with "the wonderful cool something that was flowing over my hand", which led her to learn how to communicate with words. From our viewpoint here, we can say that she grasped the concept of concept.

5 Adjectives and Adverbs

The base categorematic words we've seen so far have been derived from English nouns and verbs. Yet we'd like a way to assert that there outside the window is white snow-ing, or there in my friend's house is gentle cat-ing. Can we find a way to use adjectives and adverbs from English in our talk of the flow of all?

The phrase "white snow" tells us what kind of snow. But what difference is there from saying that there (pointing) is snow-ing and there (pointing) is whiteness? We can say "white-ing" to describe in the flow of all, viewing white-ing as a description as much as dog-ing. We can treat color words as base categorematic words which we can use to describe. In this context there is white-ing. In that context there is red-ing. Let's adopt the following as base categorematic words:

WHITE	YELLOW	BLUE
RED	BROWN	PUCE
GREEN	VIOLET	CHARTREUSE

We can use "COLOR", too, as a base categorematic word. It's more general, yet meaningful in the same way.[6]

What about "gentle"? As English speakers, we could understand six dogs or a dog running or a pack of dogs as gentle. Would that be a comparison to only other dog-ing? Surely "gentle" means the same for a gentle dog and a gentle elephant. But does it mean the same for a gentle boa constrictor? For a gentle ferris-wheel ride? To say no is, I suspect, to think of "gentle" as needing a basis for comparison —of things. But even in English we have a mass-word for the idea of being gentle: "gentleness". A problem in treating "gentle" as a modifier of predicates is how to discern a general notion of gentle from disparate uses modifying "— is a dog", "— is an elephant", "— is a boa constrictor", "— is a ferris wheel".[7] Here we can say that "gentle" gives a concept we can use in combination with other categorematic words; a comparison is not needed. We can take "GENTLE" as a base categorematic word.

Similarly, in English we have mass forms of "loud" ("loudness") and "strong" ("strength"). We can take "LOUD" and "STRONG" as base categorematic words.

We also have "beauty" as the mass form of "beautiful". So we can take "BEAUTY" as a base categorematic word. But isn't that to take beauty as a universal, independent of the kind? Yes, in thing-talk it would be. But here we are not comparing things of a kind, saying that "beautiful" is meant differently in "beautiful woman" and "beautiful dog". There is only "BEAUTY" that can be a good description of some of the flow of all. We have the concept but not necessarily an abstract or universal.

---

[6] See Appendix A for how Willard van Orman Quine, Norwood Russell Hanson, and Friedrich Waismann each came to a similar view of color terms.

[7] See *The Internal Structure of Predicates and Names*.

What about the adjective "big"? What would it mean to say that "BIG" describes in the flow of all? Is there "big-ing" here and now? We don't have in English a mass form of "big", not "bigness" for sure. If I say "Bidú is big", you'll want to know what kind of thing Bidú is. He's a dog, and yes, he's big compared to other dogs. He's an animal, and no, he's not big compared to other animals like bulls, elk, and elephants. What is big depends on the kind of things we're talking about. In the view of the world as the flow of all, there are no things and no kinds of things. "DOG" can correctly describe in the flow of all that we as speakers of English would say is two dogs, or six dogs, or a pack of dogs, or two dogs running, or . . . . What would it mean to say in such cases that "big" is a correct description? Adjectives that we use in English to compare a thing to other things of a particular kind are not suitable to adopt as categorematic words.

Words like "very", "nearly", and "almost" whose role in English is to modify other adjectives and adverbs also don't make sense to use as categorematic words. We'll consider them at the end of the next chapter.

In summary, we can adopt adjectives and adverbs from English to use as base categorematic words so long as their use and our understanding of them is not solely for comparison, as with "big", or used solely (primarily?) as modifiers of adjectives or adverbs, as with "very".

6   Categorematic Words as Modifiers

I point and say "doghouse", and you agree. "HOUSE" is a correct description in that context: there is house-ing. But "DOG" need not be a correct description: my dogs could be out running. Still, the idea, the concept of dog-ing has to be involved in the description of doghouse-ing: we can understand the compound "doghouse" only if we understand "dog". To have a categorematic word to use this way let's adopt a new notation:

HOUSE / DOG

When I assert this it's as if I were to assert "HOUSE" and say "think of dog-ing". I am saying that the concept of dog-ing is needed, involved, linked somehow to house-ing. But there need not be dog-ing there, though there could be if Birta were in the doghouse. It's hard to get this right, but it's the same problem of how to understand "dog" in "doghouse" in English, as you can see in Appendix B.

Compare:

DOG / HOUSE

I point and say this, meaning to describe what we in English call "house dogs", ones that live indoors. If in that context it's a good/accurate/correct description, then so is "DOG". But "HOUSE" need not be a correct description if the dogs are riding in a car with their heads out the window.

Modified categorematic words   If E and F are categorematic words, then E / F is a categorematic word, a *modified* categorematic word. The word F *modifies* the word E; it is the *modifier*.

> E / F is meant to evoke the concept of E in a way modified by our understanding of F; the concept elicited by F is involved with the concept of E.

> E / F is a correct description in a context iff E is a correct description in that context as modified by our understanding of F.

(I write "iff" as an abbreviation of "if and only if".)
   We already said that the conditions for a categorematic word to be a correct description follow from what concept we associate with the word. But such applications of concepts might not be clear. That is why I set out separately the conditions for a modified categorematic word to be a correct description. I'll do the same for each kind of categorematic word we consider as a guide to using such words and to better understand the notions of concepts and their use.
   From this definition we have the following, as noted in the examples above.

18   Chapter 6

If a modified categorematic word is correct, so is the word modified   If E/F is a correct description in a context, so is E.

Consider now

HOUSE / HOUSE

When I assert this it's like saying, "HOUSE" and think of the concept of "HOUSE" involved in that. Using "HOUSE" to modify itself neither adds nor subtracts to the concept.

Redundancy for modifications   We treat E/E as establishing the same concept as E, and hence E/E is a correct description in a context iff E is.

Example 1   Toy bears and bear toys.

Analysis   Speaking English I can point to a shop window and say "toy bear": that's a toy resembling or somehow meant to evoke the concept of a bear. In our talk of the flow of all we can describe with:

TOY / BEAR

At the zoo I can point to an enclosure for bears with a tire hung from a branch and say "bear toy": that's a toy meant for bears to play with. Perhaps we could use "TOY / BEAR" too, but later when we have more tools to describe we'll have better choices.

Example 2   Cartoon cat.

Analysis   Suppose I'm watching TV and I call to you and point to the screen and say "cartoon cat". In that context, "CARTOON" is a correct description, but "CAT" is not. Unless, that is, you think that cartoon cat-ing is just another kind of cat-ing. That does not seem a good way to go, no more than in our thing-conception of the world we should populate the universe with not only siamese cats and calico cats but also cartoon cats and imaginary cats. Yet the idea, the concept of cat-ing has to be involved in the description in some way, for which we can use "CARTOON/CAT".

Example 3   Fake dog.

Analysis   I have a small purple hand puppet called "Ralph" that looks like a dog (see the photo in the front matter). There, pointing, is fake-ing, imitation-ing if you like, but not dog-ing. So to describe when I point to it, I can use:

FAKE / DOG

There is fake-ing in the style of, meant to suggest, looking like, resembling in some way dog-ing. But "DOG" is not correct to assert.

Example 4 Imaginary dog.

Analysis A fellow talks when there's no one around. He says he's talking to a dog, but there's no dog there. Pressed, he says uncomfortably that he's talking to an imaginary dog. An imaginary dog is not a dog. An imaginary dog would be outside space and time, it seems. But we need not talk of an imaginary dog in that context but only of imagine-ing somehow linked to the concept of dog-ing, resembling in some way dog-ing, for which we can use:

   IMAGINE / DOG

Example 5 TOY / UNICORN

Analysis This would be correct to assert when I point to a stuffed toy that looks like what we imagine a unicorn to be. Not only is "UNICORN" not a correct description in this context, it is not a correct description in any context in the world as we know it. Yet it is useful as a modifier for it elicits a concept.

Example 6 STORY / PEGASUS

Analysis This would be a correct description of someone telling a story—and here we get into a mess in English. A story about Pegasus? What does "about Pegasus" mean if "Pegasus" does not pick out, refer to, stand for any thing, at least no thing that exists? How to talk coherently and reason about fiction is difficult in our thing language; I've worked out some ways in *The Internal Structure of Predicates and Names*. Here we can have a name like "PEGASUS" that in no context is correct to assert in the world as we know it, yet like "UNICORN" it elicits a concept for us. And "STORY/PEGASUS" can be a correct description in a context. There is no difference in how "PEGASUS" and "BIRTA" can be used. It's just that "PEGASUS" by itself never describes correctly (in the world as we know it), while in some contexts "BIRTA" does. It's really that easy in our language to have fiction talk in our talk of the flow of all.

Example 7 Competent teaching.

Analysis A mother goes to watch her child's fourth grade arithmetic class; later she says she saw competent teaching. Should we say that she saw both teaching and competence? Can there be competence-ing absent a comparison? I'm not sure. Is competence the same for teaching and for auto repair? Is it the same for ski-ing? Can we take "COMPETENCE" as a categorematic word? There are going to be lots of examples like this that will stop us. It's not just that we have to think of the concept of competence; after all, "competent" is defined in the dictionary without reference to teaching, auto repair, or ski-ing. No, the issue is how to think of competence in a view of the world as the flow of all, and for that it would be better to learn how such a concept is used in ordinary languages which lead their speakers to view the world as the flow of all.

Example 8 A dog house that's made to look like a castle.

Analysis We can describe this with:

 HOUSE/DOG/CASTLE

But this is ambiguous between:

 (HOUSE/DOG)/CASTLE

 HOUSE/(DOG/CASTLE)

We need to mark beginnings and endings of categorematic words to ensure that there's only one reading of a complex word. But in our informal discussions I'll use parentheses only when there's likely to be confusion.

Aside: Modifiers that aren't categorematic words
To say that there is very loud barking is to say that not only is the barking loud, but compared to other loud barking it is loud. It seems that "very" is used only for a comparison. How could we say (pointing or sniffing) there is very-ing? It doesn't make sense to take "very" as a base categorematic word.

 To say that Birta is nearly barking is clear enough. But how could we use "nearly" as a base categorematic word—there (pointing) is "nearly-ing"?

 To say that this pond is almost frozen is clear enough. But how could we use "almost" as a base categorematic word—there is "almost-ing"?

 There are some words from English we'd like to use as modifiers of categorematic words but not as categorematic words themselves. The categorematic words are the concept words of our language. Words such as "very", "nearly", "almost", and others are syncategorematic: they have significance only when used with a categorematic word.

 How could we use those in our language? We could write them in lower case to distinguish them from the base categorematic words. Then we could use them as modifiers with the slash notation:

 BARK/almost

 RED/nearly

 MEOW/(LOUD/very)

In this way, perhaps, we could have other modifiers that we wouldn't want to use as categorematic words, such as "fast" or "big". Then we could say "RUN/fast". These would set up comparisons: "RUN/fast" is a correct description iff running I am pointing to is fast in comparison to other running. These would also be syncategorematic.

 If we were to adopt such modifiers, we would have to divide them into restrictors and negators as with do with modifiers of predicates (see *The Internal Structure of Predicates and Names*). We would have that in any context in which "MEOW/(LOUD/very)" is a correct description, so is "(MEOW/(LOUD)", but "(BARK/almost)" could be correct while "BARK" is not. Though worth doing, that would complicate the presentation of the work here and obscure more basic points.

7   Together-Uses of Categorematic Words

I point and I mean to get you to notice that my dog Birta is running. I can say "DOG", and I can say "RUN"—both are correct. But they could be correct descriptions if (as we'd say in our thing-talk) there were a dog sleeping and a woman running. I mean to use the two descriptions as describing in some joined, mixed, together way.

It is tempting to say that the process of dog-ing and the process of run-ing are intertwined, meshed to be one process. But to talk of an intertwining or meshing is to treat "DOG" and "RUN" as names of processes. They are not names: there is only the flow of all and these words used to describe. Together "DOG" and "RUN" can be used to describe the flow of all in that context. That "together" is what distinguishes dog-running from woman-running and dog-sleeping. There is a difference between "DOG" and "RUN" applied separately or applied together as a description, and the difference in the description comes from a difference in the world.

Let's use the symbol "+" to indicate that we mean to be using categorematic words in this together-way. So we can write:

DOG + RUN

This could be a correct description of what we would call in English a dog running, or some running done by a dog, or a pack of dogs running, or simply used to elicit the concept of dog-running. Pointing to my dogs chasing a rabbit, this would be correct. Pointing to my patio now, though my dog Birta is there, it would not be correct, for she is asleep. Pointing to a marathon race with no dogs in sight, it would not be correct. Even pointing to a marathon race with a dog looking on, it would not be correct: dog-ing and running are not mixed.

I can point at an elephant and say "ELEPHANT" and that's correct. I can say "GREY", and that's correct. But more, the elephant-ing and the grey-ing are together, mixed. So "ELEPHANT + GREY" is a correct description in this context.

Similarly, "MAN + HAND" is a correct description when I to point to my friend Harry. And "CAT + MEOW" is a correct description of the cats that are keeping me awake: each of "CAT" and "MEOW" is correct to assert, and the descriptions can't be separated (even if I go out and throw a shoe at them, for then "MEOW" would no longer be correct). It seems that physical inseparability is the condition for a together use of two categorematic words to be a correct description.

When I put my shoes on in the morning I can point to my left foot and say "SHOE" and that's correct, I can say "FOOT" and that's correct. But though the shoe-ing and the foot-ing can't be pointed to separately (while I have my shoe on), we can conceptually separate them. Or perhaps we should say that we can conceptually spatially distinguish them; they are in different places, though I can't (easily) point to those. The shoe-ing and the foot-ing are not mixed, not together in a joined way. That is, "SHOE + FOOT" is not a correct description.

There is a temptation to think of a together use of categorematic words as a kind of predication: "DOG + RUN" is like asserting "A dog is running". But equally it would be correct to assert in a context of many dogs running, and it serves as a way of paying attention to the flow of all as a concept word.

Here is an example we can't construe in thing-talk:

COFFEE + WATER

This is a correct description of the mixture I get when I make coffee in the morning. All that matters is that the flow of all in this context can be described by both "COFFEE" and "WATER" together. The order of the terms doesn't matter any more than it does in "DOG + RUN": if it's correct to assert "DOG + RUN" in a context, then it's correct to assert "RUN + DOG". If it's correct to assert "COFFEE + WATER" in a context, then it's correct to assert "WATER + COFFEE".

We can make a together use of more than two categorematic words. I can describe what's in my cup when I add some sugar:

COFFEE + WATER + SUGAR

Again, there is no precedence of one of these words over the others, nor does the order matter in establishing the concept or using the word to describe, nor need we add parentheses as in "(COFFEE + WATER) + SUGAR". All three words are used together to describe in a mixed, together way, not distinguished spatially. The following are equivalent, both in establishing a concept and so in describing correctly in the flow of all.

COFFEE + WATER + SUGAR   WATER + COFFEE + SUGAR

COFFEE + SUGAR + WATER   SUGAR + WATER + COFFEE

WATER + SUGAR + COFFEE   SUGAR + COFFEE + WATER

We can combine more categorematic words still. I'll let you describe a context in which it would be correct to assert:

WIND + SMOKE + ODOR + HAZE

We can also use modified categorematic words in a together-way. For example:

HOUSE / DOG + SLEEP

But this is ambiguous. I meant it as a together-use of "HOUSE / DOG" and "SLEEP", but it could be read as "HOUSE" modified by "DOG + SLEEP". With parentheses we can make clear which of these readings is meant:

(HOUSE / DOG) + SLEEP

The parentheses are used to mark off the beginning and ending of categorematic words, not to group categorematic words in a "+" use. I'll let you use parentheses to show the various readings we can make of "SOUND / BARK + TOY / DOG".

What we mean by some mixed, or joined, or together way of describing with categorematic words will depend on the particular words that are being conjoined. We understand the together of "DOG + RUN" differently from the together of "ELEPHANT + GREY" and that differently from "WATER + COFFEE". Yet it seems to me that there is some underlying notion of two categorematic words used to describe together where they cannot be (conceptually) spatially separated in the context, though I cannot explain that well nor reduce it to any other notion.

Together-uses of categorematic words If $E, F, \ldots, H$ are categorematic words, then $E + F + \ldots + H$ is a categorematic word. It is a *together-use* of $E, F, \ldots, H$.

$E + F + \ldots + H$ is meant to evoke a concept of a mixing, joining, conceiving in a together way the concepts of $E, F, \ldots, H$.

$E + F + \ldots + H$ is a correct description in, or of, or relative to a context iff each of $E, F, \ldots, H$ is a correct description in that context, and they describe in a joined, mixed, together way in which $E, F, \ldots, H$ cannot describe as separated spatially (conceptually).

From this and our earlier discussion we have the following.

If a together-use of categorematic words is a correct description, so is each of the words that are joined If $E + F + \ldots + H$ is a correct description in a context, then each of $E, F, \ldots, H$ is correct in that context.

Order of words in a together-use doesn't matter If G is a together-use word, and G* is G with the order of the words in G re-arranged, then G* is equivalent to G both for the concept it elicits and for whether it is a correct description in a context.

Suppose Carlee, who's only two, points to my yard and excitedly says "doggy, doggy". As far as getting us to pay attention to what she sees, she could have said just "doggy". The second "doggy" emphasizes but doesn't add to the concept. So, too, "DOG + DOG" serves no purpose beyond "DOG" in eliciting a concept or as a description.

Redundancy in together-uses We treat $E + E$ as establishing the same concept as E. Hence $E + E$ is a correct description in a context iff E is a correct description in that context.

Example 1 JUSTICE + HUMAN

Analysis We can use this to describe not just the judge who is uttering "Innocent" in court but also the woman to whom he's saying it and indeed the whole courtroom, for none of those can be spatially separated from, not mixed with "JUSTICE" in this context. And in this context, each of "JUSTICE" and "HUMAN" is correct to assert, as is "HUMAN + JUSTICE".

Example 2 WIND + LEAF

Analysis This is a correct description of what we would describe in English as a leaf waving in the wind. I can't point to the wind separately, though it is correct in this context to assert "WIND".

> Who has seen the wind?
> Neither I nor you:
> But when the leaves hang trembling,
> The wind is passing through.
>
> Who has seen the wind?
> Neither you nor I:
> But when the trees bow down their heads
> The wind is passing by.
>
> Christina Rossetti

Example 3 DOG + CAT

Analysis A dog has gotten into a fierce fight with two cats. Though the dog-ing and cat-ing are related, they aren't mixed together, for the dog-ing can be distinguished spatially from the cat-ing, at least conceptually. "DOG + CAT" is not a correct description in any context. That does not rule out a cat that acts like a dog, for which we can use "CAT/DOG".

Example 4 HORSE + DONKEY

Analysis You might think this is a good description of a mule, for mule-ing is a mixture of horse-ing and donkey-ing. But that's wrong, for pointing to a mule neither "HORSE" nor "DONKEY" is a correct description.

Example 5 SWEET + SOUR

Analysis That's how I described the sauce on a fish I was eating at a Chinese restaurant. There, sweet and sour inextricably mixed.

Example 6 Tomato seeds.
        Bird seeds.

Analysis One or many tomato seeds can be correctly described with:

    TOMATO + SEED

The tomato-ing and the seed-ing are mixed, they cannot be spatially separated conceptually, and each of "TOMATO" and "SEED" is correct to assert.

To correctly describe lots of seeds in a bird feeder, with no birds around, we can use:

    SEED/BIRD

In that context "BIRD + SEED" is false, for "BIRD" is not correct to assert; the bird-ing and seed-ing are not mixed.

English grammar is no guide here.

Example 7   FAKE / DOG

FAKE + DOG

Analysis The first is a correct description of my small purple hand puppet called "Ralph" that looks like a dog. There, pointing, is fake-ing but not dog-ing. But there is not fake-ing and dog-ing mixed, for which we would use "FAKE + DOG". That would have been a correct description of the two dogs Birta and Buddy I had when I fed them. Birta would eat hurriedly then run off a little way and start barking as if there were something in that direction. Buddy, who was bigger and dominant, would then run there and start barking, and Birta would run back to eat Buddy's food while he was barking.

Example 8   TOY / (DOG + RUN)

Analysis See there, a toy that looks like a dog running. Cute, eh?

A together-use word can be a modifier.

8   Linking Categorematic Words

Suzy brought her cat Puff to Dick and Zoe's home. Spot got excited.

(1)   Puff is running from Spot.

It's wrong to ask how we can express (1) in our talk of the flow of all. That sentence construes experience in terms of things and relations between them. But we can imagine the same scene construed in the view of the world as the flow of all. We can treat the names "Puff" and "Spot" as describing Puff-ing and Spot-ing, for which we can use "PUFF" and "SPOT". Then we can describe with:

PUFF + RUN

SPOT

Each is a correct description in the flow of all at that time. But together they do not describe the scene that (1) is meant to describe because there is no "from". We need a way to use these two categorematic words in a way that they are linked in describing, though not in a mixed or together way. Let's make a new word:

(2)   PUFF + RUN <u>from</u> SPOT

For this to be a correct description, the concept we have of "PUFF + RUN" must be linked with the concept we have of "SPOT" in a way we understand with "<u>from</u>". We need some understanding of "<u>from</u>", though not to use as a correct or incorrect description, which is why I underline it. Rather, it is a *categorematic linking*, meant to join categorematic words to form a new word to elicit a concept that arises from linking concepts of the words it joins.

With (2) we have a word we can use to describe in the flow of all. We can form the conception without knowing whether the categorematic words that are linked in it are correct or incorrect, for that question arises only when we have indicated context. The concept comes first; applying it in context then follows. But we can say that for (2) to be a correct description in context, each of the categorematic words that are linked, "PUFF + RUN" and "SPOT", must be correct, too.

Can't we say more about how (2) is a correct description? If someone proposes to use "<u>from</u>" as a linking of categorematic words, it's because he or she assumes that we understand "<u>from</u>" well enough to recognize whether (2) is a correct description. There may be no simpler notions in terms of which it can be explained.

The claim (2) is an incomplete description of that scene. In thing-talk, a fuller description is:

(3)   Puff is running from Spot barking.

We can describe this with:

(4)   (PUFF + RUN) <u>from</u> (SPOT + BARK)

Suppose further that where (4) is correct to assert,

    Puff is running into some bushes.

To describe this, we can use "(PUFF + RUN) <u>into</u> BUSH". And to describe "Suzy is running with Puff", we can use "(SUZY + RUN) <u>with</u> PUFF". And to describe my foot in a shoe, we can use "(FOOT) <u>in</u> (SHOE)".

    Suppose in the scene described at (3),

(5)   Dick is watching Spot barking.

There is no preposition in (5) we can borrow from English to use for a linking. Yet as with the other examples, some linking of the concepts of Dick-watching and Spot-barking must hold for (5) to be correct. From our thing-talk we might adopt "<u>directed towards</u>" and then have:

    (DICK + WATCH) <u>directed towards</u> (SPOT + BARK)

And we can describe Spot looking to where he heard a cat meow:

(6)   DOG <u>directed towards</u> MEOW

    Note that the order of the words can matter in a linked categorematic word. Though (6) is a correct description in this context, "MEOW <u>directed towards</u> DOG" may be false.

Compounding categorematic linkings

Suppose that at the scene described in (1),

(7)   Suzy sees Puff running from Spot.

We can use the following for what (7) is meant to describe:

(8)   (SUZY + SEE) <u>directed towards</u> ((PUFF + RUN) <u>from</u> (SPOT + BARK))

    What does that mean? The word (2) describes a nexus, a view of the flux under distinct descriptions. The word (8) describes a larger nexus. With considerable risk of being misleading, I'll try to picture what (8) describes.

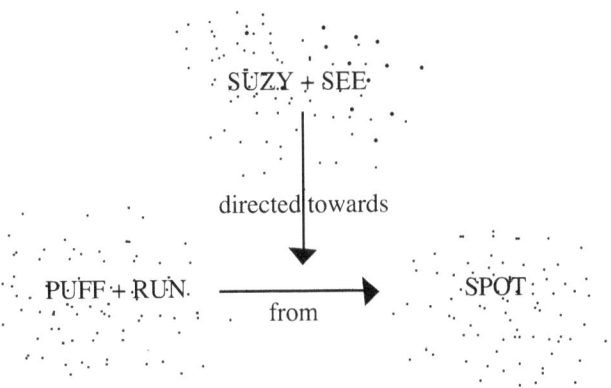

We have (8) as a way to describe and then ask if that concept yields a correct description in this context. To do this we allow a linked categorematic word to be linked with a categorematic word. For simplicity, let's consider linkings of only two categorematic words here, either of which could be a linked word.

Linking categorematic words A *categorematic linking* $\underline{c}$ is a way to join any two categorematic words E and F to make a new categorematic word E $\underline{c}$ F.

E $\underline{c}$ F is meant to evoke the concept of E linked with the concept of F in a way peculiar to our understanding of $\underline{c}$.

E $\underline{c}$ F is a correct description in a context iff each of E and F is a correct description in that context and the two words describe together correctly in a way particular to this linking.

By this definition, + is a categorematic linking. And just as with +, in the examples above if a linking of words is a correct description in a context each of the words linked has to be correct in that context. But if we require that, then we can't use "(SUZY + THINK) of UNICORN" to describe Suzy thinking of a unicorn, for in no context is "UNICORN" correct. Yet if Puff is in the room with her, we might correctly assert "(SUZY + AWARE) of PUFF". The problem is not with the linking "of" but with "THINK" and "AWARE", both of which are closely tied to our thing-conception of the world. So I propose that we adopt the following, leaving to others to sort out how to use those words.

If a linking of categorematic words is a correct description, so are the words linked
If E $\underline{c}$ F is a correct description in a context, so are E and F.

Aside: Prepositions as linkings
I've used prepositions "from", "in", "into", "with" for linkings. These are peculiar to English and cannot be translated clearly into other languages. Stephen C. Levinson in "Relativity in Spatial Conception and Description" says that the Mayan language Tzeltal has only one preposition. Perhaps we could adopt an all-purpose linking "§" to supplement the linking "+" that we already have. Then if someone asserts "HORSE § TREE", we'd ask for some explanation of how she means for us to construe "§" linking concepts, just as we ask Spanish speakers to explain how we're to understand their all-purpose preposition "de".

9 Disjoining Categorematic Words

My friend says his corral is for horses and donkeys. Sometimes donkeys are there, sometimes a horse, sometimes both, sometimes neither. It's what we might call a horse-donkey corral. Let's coin a new word to describe in the flow of all:

   HORSE – DONKEY

This is meant to evoke the concepts of both "HORSE" and "DONKEY" not mixed or together but either-or. It's a correct description in the context of the corral iff either "HORSE" or "DONKEY" is a correct description or both are. Using this new word we can describe my friend's corral:

   CORRAL / (HORSE – DONKEY)

   At dusk I see some large shapes in his corral. I can't discern if they're horses or donkeys or some horses and some donkeys. But I know I'm correct to assert "HORSE – DONKEY" because either "HORSE" is a correct description or "DONKEY" is a correct description or both are. Equally, "DONKEY – HORSE" would be a correct description. The order of the categorematic words doesn't matter.

   A fellow I know is color-blind. He can't consistently use "RED" correctly; he can't consistently use "GREEN" correctly. But he's almost always right when he asserts "RED – GREEN".

   I go for a walk and see my dog Arfito running fast next to the irrigation canal and then across a field trying to catch something. I see it from a distance for only a second yet enough for me to confidently assert:

   (ARFITO + CHASE) <u>directed towards</u> (SQUIRREL – GOPHER)

That's the best description I can make, since he didn't catch it. And it's useful, for it may be the first step in my finding out what his chasing was directed towards.

   Suppose that my friend has acquired a mule now, and he puts her into his horse-donkey corral. It's now a horse-donkey-corral. We can say that in our talk:

   CORRAL / (HORSE – DONKEY – MULE)

We have the word:

   (HORSE – DONKEY – MULE)

This is a correct description in a context iff either "HORSE" or "DONKEY" or "MULE" is a correct description in that context. So the following are equivalent in establishing a concept and hence in describing correctly in the flow of all.

HORSE – DONKEY – MULE	DONKEY – HORSE – MULE
HORSE – MULE – DONKEY	MULE – DONKEY – HORSE
DONKEY – MULE – HORSE	MULE – HORSE – DONKEY

Disjoining categorematic words   If E, F, ..., H are categorematic words, then E – F – ... – H is a categorematic word. It is a *disjoining* of E, F, ..., H.

> E – F – ... – H is meant to evoke the concept of E, and the concept of F, ..., and the concept of H as alternatives, not in a linked or together way.
>
> E – F – ... – H is a correct description in a context iff E is a correct description in the context, or F is a correct description in the context, ..., or H is a correct description in the context.

Note that this does not rule out that more than one of the disjoined words is correct in the context. It would be correct to assert "HORSE – DONKEY – MULE" for the context of my friend's corral if there were a horse and three donkeys there.

I'll let you convince yourself of the following.

Order of words in a disjoining doesn't matter   If G is a a disjoining of categorematic words, and G* is G with the order of the words in G re-arranged, then G* is equivalent to G both for the concept it elicits and for whether it is a correct description in context.

A disjoining is more general than the words disjoined   If E is a correct description in context, and G is a disjoining of categorematic words in which E appears, then G is a correct description in that context.

Redundancy in disjoinings   E – E is equivalent to E for the concept it elicits and so also for whether it is a correct description in a context.

10 Negative Categorematic Words

How can we say in the context of my yard some dog-ing is not sleeping?
    We have no way to say "not" or "no". We need a word that we can use to describe not-sleeping. Let's use:

   non-SLEEP

This is a categorematic word, meant to describe in context. Pointing to tree-ing in the context, it's a correct description.. Together with "DOG" we can say some dog-ing is not sleeping:

   DOG + (non-SLEEP)

Dog-ing is mixed inextricably with non-sleep-ing. See Arfito alert and looking around.

***non*-E**   If E is a categorematic word E, then non-E is a categorematic word. It is a *negating* of E.

   non-E is meant to evoke the concept: absence of E.

   non-E is a correct description in context iff in some of the context
   E does not describe correctly

I've added "in some of the context" here, though that's so for all our categorematic words, each of which is meant to describe correctly some though not necessarily all the context. "DOG + (non-SLEEP)" is correct in the context of my yard though another dog is sleeping while Arfito is not.

Example 1   DOG + (non-GREYHOUND)
Analysis   I don't know what kind of dog this is, but I'm sure it's not a greyhound.
    This example could also be used as a description of a pack of chihuahuas on the hunt. Or it could be used to describe correctly in a context with a couple of cocker spaniels playing with a greyhound.

Example 2   (non-DOG)
Analysis   You say "COYOTE". I say "non-DOG". How do we know we're talking about the same? "non-DOG" by itself tells us very little and is a correct description in many contexts, even when "DOG" is correct.

Example 3   TOY / (non-DOG)
Analysis   Those are not toy dogs, they're toy wolves. Can't you see?
    For this to be a correct description, "TOY" has to be correct and we're to understand that word as somehow involved, completed with the concept of non-dog-ing.

Here "non-DOG" is not meant as a description; only the concept of "non-DOG" is involved. Another toy that looks like a poodle could be on the same shelf and the example would still be correct.

Example 4 HOUSE / (non-DOG)

Analysis This would be a correct description if in context there's a house not meant for a dog or perhaps a house where no dog is allowed inside.

Example 5 non-(non-TOY)

Analysis For "non-(non-TOY)" to be a correct description, "non-TOY" has to be incorrect in some of the context. That is, in some of the context, "TOY" is a correct description. That is, "non-(non-TOY)" is correct description in context iff "TOY" is correct.

Non-non non-(non-E) is a correct description in a context iff E is a correct description in the context.

This is not to say that non-(non-E) is meant to elicit the same concept as E. Non-non-toy-ing is not conceptually the same as toy-ing. Or at least it isn't for me.

Example 6 DOG – (non-DOG)

Analysis This is a correct description in the context of my corral: there, locally, either dog-ing or absence of dog-ing. Generally we have the following.

E or non-E For any categorematic word E, in any context, E – (non-E) is a correct description.

Example 7 (non-DOG) / HOUSE

Analysis Suppose in front of my home a friend says "non-DOG". There where she's looking there is tree-ing, wind-ing, dirt-ing, dog-ing, sky-ing, sun-ing, ... If she had said, "TREE" she would have led me to focus my attention with her. But a negative categorematic word requires further pointing for us to evaluate it, perhaps using an additional categorematic word in the description.

If my friend then asserts "(non-DOG) / HOUSE", I have no idea what she intends me to pay attention to: see, not-dog-ing and think of house-ing? It's not that it elicits no concept. It can't lead me to pay attention jointly with her, and I can find no way to evaluate it. So I'm not justified in saying it's a correct description. Nor is she justified in saying it's correct, at least not without supplementing it in some way. And it's not just this context. In any context "(non-DOG) / HOUSE" cannot be used to make a correct description. Hence, in any context it's not a correct description.

Null words A word is *null* if the concept it elicits does not allow for it to be used to describe correctly in any context. A null word word describes incorrectly in every context.

Example 8 CAT − ((non-DOG) / HOUSE)

Analysis "(non-DOG) / HOUSE" is a null word. Hence, the example is a correct description in a context iff "CAT" is a correct description in the context.

We need some justification to say that a word describes correctly in a context, whether by pointing, discussing with one another what concept it elicits, ... If we have no pointing, the word is not correct: that a description is incorrect is our default judgment.

Example 9 (non-(non-TOY)) / DOG

Analysis Recall that for any categorematic words E and F,

> E / F is meant to evoke the concept of E in a way modified by our understanding of F

As we noted above, "non-(non-TOY)" is not meant to elicit the same concept as "TOY". So "(non-(non-TOY)) / DOG" is not meant to elicit the same concept as "TOY / DOG". But since "non-(non-TOY)" is a correct description in context iff "TOY" is, in any context the two words either both describe correctly or neither does.

Example 10 CAT + ((non-DOG) / HOUSE)

Analysis Since "(non-DOG) / HOUSE" is null, the example cannot be a correct description in a context.

How can we tell if a word is null? It's not obvious by form, since both "(non-DOG) / HOUSE" and "(non-(non-TOY)) / DOG" have the form (non-E)/F. Nor can knowing "the" concept that it elicits suffice. A child can acquire a concept for "UNICORN" but still be disappointed when she later learns that it is not a correct description in any context. Often enough we discover that a word is not a correct description in any context only by using it.

Summary

Our categorematic words play three roles:

- They are meant to elicit concepts for us.
- Through those concepts we understand how they can be used to describe in the flow of all.
- We use them to describe.

pointing and saying a categorematic word intending to describe = *asserting*

By "pointing" I mean any way we try to get someone to pay attention jointly with us.

If I utter "DOG", "MUD", "RUN" in a context, and these describe correctly, and you know the words, and each word elicits "a" concept for you that is like enough to "the" concept it elicits for me, then by asserting we can pay attention together. That, too, is pointing.

I point at the field I see outside my window and say "GRASS". I correctly describe — not all of the context, but some. What grass-ing? The word points our attention to all grass-ing in the context. That's not all of the context, for there is also dirt-ing and weed-ing and fence-ing. To assert is to assert locally, though the grass-ing may be in many different places in the field. I assert "DOG" and that's correct because Arfito and one of his doggy friends are there in the field, running around. It's a local assertion because it's meant to focus on only dog-ing. All our descriptions using categorematic words are meant as *local*.

correctly describing = correctly describing some of the context

Sometimes asserting a word correctly does describe all in the context. If we take as context drift of snow in my yard, "SNOW" describes correctly all, and so does "WHITE". But that's unusual and not useful because there is nothing in the context to distinguish from "SNOW" or to distinguish from "WHITE".

We also have ways to form complex categorematic words for "fuller" descriptions, directing attention more finely, distinguishing more. With "GRASS + GREEN" we can narrow what we are paying attention to, for there may be dead brown grass-ing in the context. With "DOG + (non-BROWN)" we can narrow what we are paying attention to, for there may be a black and white dog there as well as a brown one.

If I use a word which you don't know, or which elicits a concept differently for you than it does for me, then even if I assert correctly I haven't directed your attention: we can't pay attention jointly. Sitting in front of my house, surveying the fields and irrigation canals, I say "GURGLE". You don't have a clue what I'm saying. But I've described correctly, for water is running from the canal into the field making a bubbling sound. You can't pay attention jointly to what I'm describing, for you don't know if I'm trying to get you to pay attention to sky-ing, dog-ing, alfalfa-ing, canal-ing, water-ing, sound, color, smell, ... You look at me quizzically and say "COLOR". How can I say you're wrong? I can lead you over to the sluice where the water flows from the canal to the field, cup my ear, and point. I can even say "SOUND". Perhaps then you'll understand "GURGLE". Or perhaps not. Gestures are unreliable without shared concepts.

We need a way not only to direct attention but also to say what is an incorrect description. We need a new kind of word for denying rather than asserting.

Compound Words

11 Compound Words

Global negation

What if someone asserts incorrectly? A friend and I were standing outside the corral at my ranch Dogshine a few years ago—that's the context. Recall the picture so you can be with us in our describing.

She asserts "GOAT". That's wrong. No goat-ing there. Those are Barbados sheep, no wool, bred to live in hot climates. Though she has not described correctly, I can guess what she means to describe, and I figure I'll correct her by asserting "SHEEP". But how does she know that this is a correction? Since "SHEEP" and "GOAT" elicit similar concepts perhaps she can figure it out. But maybe she thinks "SHEEP" correctly describes because there is some sheep-ing alongside the goat-ing in the corral. I can't say she's wrong about that (what she thought was goat-ing but really is sheep-ing) except to use a correct description. With our categorematic words I can direct her attention using only *positive* descriptions, and that won't help because a correct positive description does not eliminate, it only focuses attention to what it correctly describes. Even "non-GOAT" is a positive description in that it focuses our attention to what is non-goat-ing in the context: chicken-ing, wood-ing, ...

Perhaps I could point and say "GOAT" and shake my head "no". Gestures are an important part of how we communicate, but I'll not try to incorporate a study of them here.[8]

How can we assert that someone is wrong when we can't focus attention in the context to what she's wrong about?

We can make a *global* description. No goat-ing anywhere in the context. For that let's write: ¬ (GOAT). No goat-ing. This is not meant to be a categorematic

---

[8] See my book *Conventional Gestures: Meaning and methodology*.

word: it elicits no concept except through the incorporation of "GOAT". It does not describe locally. But it can describe correctly or incorrectly. When it does describe correctly it does not point our attention jointly in the context, it only eliminates a description.

All our words so far have been categorematic, meant for positive descriptions. "¬ (GOAT)" is a *negation*, "no GOAT"; it is a *compound* word meant as a *global* description in a context.

Global negation   Given any word E, ¬ (E) is a *compound* word. It is a correct description in a context iff E is not a correct description. It is not meant to elicit a concept.

We pronounce "¬ (E)" as "no E".

---

   asserting ¬ (E) in context = *denying* E

From this definition we have:

   ¬ (E) is a correct description in a context iff
   none of the context is correctly described with E

When meant to deny in the context of looking at a patch of mud in my patio, "¬ (BLUE)" is correct: no blue-ing there. When denying in the context of the area in front of the house where I live, "¬ (DOG)" is incorrect, for in some of the context "DOG" is a correct description, but "¬ (DOG + SLEEP)" is correct as the dogs are running around.

Conjunction

If "¬ (TOY / DOG)" is a correct description, it doesn't tell us much. It doesn't focus our attention jointly; it just denies. It could be correct if "TOY" doesn't describe correctly in the context. Or it could be correct if "TOY" does describe correctly but doesn't when the concept of "DOG" is with it. Look: it's a toy wolf. For that couldn't we use "TOY / ¬ (DOG)"? No, because "¬ (DOG)" is not a categorematic word; it's not meant to elicit a concept. We can say that "TOY" is a correct description but "TOY / DOG" is not if we use both those words together to describe: TOY ∧ ¬ (TOY / DOG).

Conjunctions   Given any words E and F, E ∧ F is a *compound* word. It is a correct description in a context iff E is a correct description in the context and F is a correct description in the context. It is not meant to elicit a concept.

We read "E ∧ F" as "E and F".

Suppose that Arfito and a couple of his doggy friends are playing in front of my home. I say "ARFITO" and my friend wonders what that's meant to describe. Is it the brown dog? Is it the car? If she thinks "ARFITO" is meant to describe my grey car, she might try asserting:

(ARFITO + CAR + GREY)

I can tell her she's wrong by asserting:

(1)   ¬ (ARFITO + CAR + GREY)

But that doesn't tell her what I want her to pay attention to, only what Arfito-ing isn't.

Knowing that (1) is correct narrows very little how my friend might conceive of "ARFITO". It's like children playing twenty-questions and learning that it's not a car, not brown, not bigger than a breadbasket, . . . until there's nothing left for her to focus on except the black and white dog. Except there is always more to focus on: the grass, the dirt, the table, the sky, ... Nothing in our talk in the flow of all restricts her conceiving to what we would call individual things. But I can direct her attention correctly by using:

(2)   (ARFITO + DOG) ∧ ¬ (ARFITO + BROWN)

Or at least I can if there's no other non-brown-ing dog-ing there. A negative description can help direct our attention only when conjoined with a positive description.

Some examples will, I hope, make clearer how we can use compound words and how they differ from categorematic words.

12 Examples

Example 1   (non-BROWN)
         ¬ (BROWN)

Analysis   As descriptions in the context of a patch of mud in my patio both are incorrect because all the mud is brown.

Example 2   (non-GREEN)
         ¬ (GREEN)

Analysis   Both of these are correct as descriptions of that patch of mud in my patio. But they are different. The first is an assertion that some of the mud is non-green. The second is correct only if all the mud is non-green.

Example 3   (non-DOG)
         ¬ (DOG)

Analysis   As descriptions of the area in front of my home, the first is correct: see, table-ing, tree-ing, ... But the second is incorrect because in some of the context "DOG" is correct: see, Arfito-ing there.

   If looking outside my office window at the field I say "¬ DOG" and that's correct, then you know that no matter where you look in that context there's no dog-ing there. So "(non-DOG)" is correct, too. This holds generally.

If no E, then non-E   For any categorematic word E, in any context, if ¬ E is a correct description, so is non-E.

   But as we just saw, non-E can be a correct description in a context in which ¬ E is not a correct description.

Example 4   PARROT + (non-GREEN)
         ¬ (PARROT + GREEN)

Analysis   The first would be a correct description if we saw a blue parrot or a flock of red parrots in a jungle along with a green parrot. "PARROT" establishes a local pointing, and in the context established by that, "non-GREEN" is correct.
   Then someone in our group points and says "PARROT + GREEN". Our guide knows he's wrong. So she rules that out by asserting "¬ (PARROT + GREEN)". There isn't any parrot-ing mixed with green-ing in the context of the jungle where we are, which includes where he's pointing. That would also be correct if there's no parrot-ing at all in that context.

Example 5   non-(DOG + CAT)
         ¬ (DOG + CAT)

Analysis "DOG + CAT" is never a correct description, for dog-ing can always be (conceptually) spatially separated from cat-ing. So both of these are correct descriptions in any context.

Example 6 (non-DOG) <u>directed towards</u> CAT

⌐ (DOG <u>directed towards</u> CAT)

Analysis The first could be correct if there are two dogs directed towards a cat and a sparrow alert and wary directed towards that cat, too. However, the second would be incorrect, for it would rule out any dog-ing directed towards cat-ing.

Example 7 CAT − (non-DOG)

Analysis   I can't figure out why we'd want to use this. The example doesn't deny "(CAT − DOG)" because it's a local description. But it's not null.

Example 8 ⌐ (⌐ (CAT))

Analysis This is a correct description iff "⌐ (CAT)" is not correct. "⌐ (CAT)" is not a correct description iff "CAT" is a correct description. And this is iff in some of the context, "CAT" describes correctly. That is, "⌐ (⌐ (CAT))" is a correct description in a context iff "CAT" is.

Example 9 ⌐ (⌐ (CAT ∧ ⌐ DOG))

Analysis This is a correct description iff "⌐ (CAT ∧ ⌐ DOG)" is not correct, which is iff "CAT ∧ ⌐ DOG" is a correct description.

No-no For any word E, categorematic or compound, and any context, ⌐ (⌐ E) is a correct description iff E is a correct description.

Example 10 ⌐ (DOG + CHASE <u>directed towards</u> CAT)

Analysis If someone asserts this, and it's correct, then it sort of focuses our attention because some of the flow got the person to make this denial, and I can probably guess what the person intends to deny. But that's vague and uncertain. Similarity is not good enough to rely on for directing our attention jointly. This is a denial, not a positive description.

Example 11 ⌐ (HORSE − DONKEY)

Analysis If you assert this and it's correct, it doesn't focus our attention jointly. It's just says that in all of the context both "HORSE" and "DONKEY" are not correct descriptions.

Example 12   ⌐ ((⌐ DOG) ∧ (⌐ CAT))

Analysis We have in any context:

"¬ ((¬ DOG) ∧ (¬ CAT))" is a correct description iff

"(¬ DOG) ∧ (¬ CAT)" is not a correct description iff

"¬ DOG" is not a correct description or "¬ CAT" is not a correct description iff

"DOG" is a correct description or "CAT" is a correct description

---

Disjunction For any words E and F, categorematic or compound,

E ∨ F ≡$_{Def}$ ¬ (¬ E ∧ ¬ F)

E ∨ F is a correct description in a context iff E is a correct description or F is a correct description.

Example 13   DOG – CAT

Analysis This is a correct description in a context iff in some of the context "DOG" is a correct description or "CAT" is a correct description. And that's iff in the context "DOG" is a correct description or "CAT" is a correct description.

– is equivalent to ∨ for describing For any categorematic words E and F, for any context, E – F is a correct description iff E ∨ F is a correct description.

But we still need local disjoining to say "TOY / (DOG – WOLF)".

Example 14   (GRASS + GREEN) ∧ ¬ (GRASS + GREEN)

(GRASS + GREEN) ∧ (GRASS + non-GREEN)

Analysis The first is not a correct description in any context: there cannot be green-ing mixed with grass-ing and complete absence of green-ing mixed with grass-ing. But the second can be a correct description: look, in that field there is green-ing grass-ing, and there is non-green-ing grass-ing, see that sere brown grass?

Example 15   ¬ (DOG ∧ (¬ DOG))

Analysis If "DOG" is correct in a context, then it describes correctly in the context. If "¬ (DOG)" is correct in a context, then "DOG" is not a correct description in the context. So "DOG ∧ ¬ (DOG)" cannot be correct in a context. So in any context, "¬ (DOG ∧ ¬ (DOG))" is a correct description.

---

noncontradiction For any word E, categorematic or compound, in any context ¬ (E ∧ (¬ E)) is a correct description.

Example 16   ¬ (DOG ∧ (¬ BARK))

Analysis We have in any context:

"¬ (DOG ∧ (¬ BARK))" is a correct description iff

"DOG ∧ (¬ BARK)" is not a correct description iff

"DOG" is not a correct description or
    "¬ BARK" is not a correct description iff

"DOG" is not a correct description or
    "BARK" is a correct description iff

if "DOG" is a correct description in the context,
    then "BARK" is a correct description in the context.

⊃   For any words E and F, categorematic or compound,

$E \supset F \equiv_{Def} \neg (E \wedge \neg F)$

In any context, E ⊃ F is a correct description iff
   if E is a correct description, then F is a correct description.

We read "⊃" as "hook", or informally as "if ... then ...".

Example 17   CAT ∨ ((non-DOG)/ HOUSE)

Analysis   In Example 7 of Chapter 10 we agreed that "((non-DOG)/ HOUSE)" is null. So this is a correct description in a context iff "CAT" is a correct description.

    We could investigate more examples. But coming up with new examples is not enough. We need a general guide for forming and evaluating words.

Form and Content

13 Forms of Words

Vocabulary

- *Base categorematic words*
- *Local connectives* /, +, −, non-, categorematic linkings
- *Global connectives* ¬, ∧
- *Parentheses* ( )

Categorematic words

A *base* word is one in which no other vocabulary appears.
Each base word is a categorematic word.

We form *complex* categorematic words starting with the base words in the following ways.

- For any categorematic words E and F, (E/F) is a categorematic word.
  It is a *modified* categorematic word; F is the *modifier* which *modifies* E.
  Each of E, F, and / *appears in* (E/F).

- For any categorematic words E, F, ..., H, (E + F + ... + H) is a categorematic word. It is a *together-use* of E, F, ..., H.
  Each of E, F, ..., H and + *appears in* (E + F + ... + H).

- For any categorematic words E and F and categorematic linking c̲,
  (E c̲ F) is a categorematic word. It is a *linking of E and F by* c̲.
  Each of E, F, and c̲ *appears in* (E c̲ F).

- For any categorematic words E, F, ..., H , (E − F − ... − H) is a categorematic word. It is a *disjoining* of E, F, ..., H.
  Each of E, F, ..., H, and − *appears in* it.

- For any categorematic word E, (non-E) is a categorematic word.
  It is an *negating* of E.
  Each of E and non- *appears in* (non-E).

Compound words

- For any categorematic word E, (¬ E) is a compound word.
  It is a *negative* word. Each of E and ¬ *appears in* (¬ E).

- For any categorematic words E and F, (E ∧ F) is a compound word.
  It is a *conjunction*. Each of E, F, and ∧ *appears in* (E ∧ F).

- For any word A, categorematic or compound, (¬ A) is a compound word.
  It is a *negative* word. Each of A and ¬ *appear in* (¬ A).

- For any words A and B, categorematic or compound, (A ∧ B) is a compound word. It is a *conjunction*. Each of A, B, and ∧ *appears in* (A ∧ B).

We'll assume throughout:

   E, F, G, H, K   stand for categorematic words.

   A, B, C, D   stand for any words, categorematic or compound.

If a word, or linking, or connective appears in A, and A appears in B, then the word, or linking, or connective *appears in* B.

Recall two definitions from Chapter 12:

   A ∨ B ≡$_{Def}$ ¬(¬A ∧ ¬B)

   A ⊃ B ≡$_{Def}$ ¬(A ∧ ¬B)

Schemes of words

Word schemes Any concatenation of upper-case letters, lower-case letters, local connectives, global connectives, and parentheses according to the rules for forming words is a *scheme* of words. It is a *compound word scheme* if only ¬, ∧, and upper-case letters appear in it.

Instantiation of a scheme An *instantiation* of a word scheme is the result of both:
- Replacing each lower-case letter in it with a categorematic linking, where every occurrence of a lower-case letter in the scheme is replaced by the same categorematic linking.
- Replacing each upper-case letter in it with a word, categorematic if flanked by a local connective, where every occurrence of an upper-case letter in the scheme is replaced by the same word.

We call an instantiation of a scheme an *instance* of the scheme.

Example 1 ((E + F) / G)

   ((¬ (F − G)) ∧ (G / H))

   ((F c̲ E) − (G + H))

Analysis Each of these is a scheme of words.

Example 2 (A ∧ B) ∧ ¬ C

   ((E / F) ∧ G) ∧ ¬ (D / E)

Analysis The first is a compound word scheme. The second is not.

Example 3 (((¬ E) + F) / G)

Analysis This is not a scheme of words: The rule for forming a word with + requires that the words being joined are categorematic, and no word of the form ¬ E is categorematic.

Example 4 (E + F) / G

Analysis This is not a scheme of words. A parenthesis is missing before the concatenation and another after it.

But lots of parentheses can make it hard to read schemes and words. So informally I'll leave off parentheses before and after a concatenation or a word if it seems likely there will be no misunderstanding. So we can understand this example as an abbreviation of the first scheme of Example 1.

Example 5 (E – F) ∧ (¬ E)

Analysis The following is an instantiation of this scheme of words:

(CAT – RAIN) ∧ (¬ CAT)

The following are not instantiations of it:

(CAT – RAIN) ∧ (¬ RAIN)

(CAT – RAIN) ∧ (¬ DOG)

But the following is an instantiation of the example:

(CAT – CAT) ∧ (¬ CAT)

We do not require that different letters be replaced by different words.

The following is also an instantiation of the example:

((CAT + RUN) – (DOG + RUN)) ∧ (¬ (CAT + RUN))

A letter can be replaced by a complex or compound word. But if the letter is flanked by a local connective, it must be replaced with a categorematic word.

Example 6 (E ∨ F)

Analysis The following is an instantiation of this scheme of words:

(DOG ∨ CAT)

Written out in full, this is: ¬ (¬ (DOG) ∧ ¬ (CAT)).

The following is also an instantiation:

(DOG ∧ HORSE) ∨ (WIND + LEAF)

Example 7 ((H c̲ K) ∧ (¬(E d̲ F)) ∧ (T e̲ W)

Analysis The following is an instantiation of this scheme of words:

((DOG <u>directed towards</u> MEAT) ∧ (¬ ((HORSE + RUN) <u>from</u> DOG)))

∧ ((MAN – WOMAN) <u>with</u> CAT))

(I'm using the convention that we can continue writing a word on a second line.)

Again there is no requirement that a letter has to be replaced by a base word.

The following is also a instantiation of the example:

((DOG <u>with</u> MEAT) ∧ ¬((HORSE + RUN) <u>with</u> DOG))

∧ ((MAN − WOMAN) <u>with</u> CAT))

There is no requirement that different lower-case letters have to be replaced by different categorematic linkings.

Example 8 (E + F) − (E / G)

Analysis The following is not an instantiation of this example:

(FLY + (RUN ∧ CAR)) − (FLY / DOG)

The replacement of F is not a categorematic word, so "(FLY + (RUN ∧ CAR))" is not allowed by the formation rules.

Now we can make clearer that the formation rules determine the structures of all words.

Every word is an instantiation of some scheme Any concatenation is a word iff there is some word scheme of which it is an instance.

Sometimes we want to instantiate several schemes together. Consider:

(1)   E + F

   ¬ F

   E

Nothing we've said would rule out instantiating these schemes with:

(2)   HORSE + RUN

   ¬ WALK

   CAT

But we mean for the restrictions on replacements to apply to all of the letters at (1) together. So any upper-case letter that appears in one of the schemes should be replaced by the same word in all of the schemes, and any lower-case letter that appears in one of the schemes should be replaced by the same categorematic linking in all of the schemes. That is, the instantiations should be *compatible*. The instantiations of (1) at (2) are not compatible, but the following are:

   HORSE + RUN

   ¬ RUN

   HORSE

And so are:

(HORSE + NEIGH) – (CAT – DOG)

¬ (CAT – DOG)

(HORSE + NEIGH)

Compatible instantiations of schemes Given two or more schemes of words, instantiations of those are compatible if any upper-case letter that appears in one of the schemes is replaced by the same word in all the schemes, and any lower-case letter that appears in one of the schemes is replaced by the same categorematic linking in all the schemes.

Example 9 E $\underline{c}$ F

G $\underline{c}$ D

Analysis These instantiations of the schemes are not compatible:

RUN <u>directed towards</u> HOUSE

LOOK <u>at</u> DOG

Different categorematic linkings replace $\underline{c}$ in the first and second.

These are compatible instantiations of the example:

(RUN + MAN) <u>directed towards</u> (HOUSE + FIRE)

(WATER + HOSE) <u>directed towards</u> FIRE

Any replacement that isn't prohibited is allowed. However, for a particular scheme or schemes we might stipulate that we require that different letters be replaced by different words or different linkings.

Aside: A formal language?
There are two reasons I have not defined a formal language for the structure of words.
   First, thing-talk is crucial for defining by induction on the length of a formal word or for talking of collections of words, which are the only ways I know to make such a definition.
   The second problem arises not only here but in all presentations of modern formal logic that I've seen, including my own work. To present a formal logic we have to use "meta-variables" to stand for formal words, as when we say "If A and B are formal words, then A ∧ B is a formal word". Doing so we employ an unexamined use of schemes of words. We could avoid that if we were to formalize the use of meta-variables. But then we would have to use meta-meta-variables and we're off to an infinite hierarchy of formal languages. Here I stop at the first level with an extensive but informal discussion of schemes.

14 How Words Elicit Concepts and Can Be Used to Describe

We start with some base categorematic words and categorematic linkings. These are not meant to comprise a fixed list but can be added in our talk.

Concepts elicited by words

Base categorematic words
Each base categorematic word is meant to elicit a concept.

> Though for each of us a base categorematic word elicits a concept differently from how it elicits a concept for anyone else, we assume that we can calibrate our use of words and concepts so that we understand sufficiently alike to be able to communicate, that is, find our way in the world together.

Complex categorematic words

- E/F is meant to evoke the concept of E in a way modified by our understanding of F; the concept elicited by F is involved, completed somehow with the concept of E.
- E + F + ... + H is meant to evoke the concept of a mixing, joining, in some together way the concepts of E, F, ..., H.
- E $\underline{c}$ F is meant to evoke the concept of E linked with the concept of F in a way peculiar to our understanding of $\underline{c}$.
- E – F – ... – H is meant to evoke the concept of E, and the concept of F, ..., and the concept of H as alternatives, not in a linked or together way.
- non-E is meant to evoke the concept of non-E, the absence of E.

Compound words
No compound word is meant to elicit a concept.

Describing correctly with words

Categorematic words
Whether a categorematic word describes correctly in a context is determined by the concept the word elicits. For base categorematic words this is taken as given and is meant to be understood as describing correctly in some but not necessarily all the context.

The concept elicited by a complex word determines whether it is a correct description in a context in the following ways.

- E/F is a correct description in a context iff E is a correct description in a way modified by our understanding of F.

- E + F + ... + H is a correct description in a context iff each of E, F, ..., H is a correct description in the context and they describe in a joined, mixed, together way in which E, F, ..., H cannot be (conceptually) separated spatially.

- E c F is a correct description in a context iff E is a correct description and F is a correct description, and the two words describe together in a way peculiar to this linking.

- E – F – ... – H is a correct description in a context iff E is a correct description, or F is a correct description, ..., or H is a correct description.

- non-E is a correct description in a context iff in some of the context E does not describe correctly.

Compound words

- ⌐ A is a correct description in a context iff A is not a correct description in the context. That is, in none of the context is A a correct description.

- A ∧ B is a correct description in a context iff A is a correct description in some of the context and B is a correct description in some of the context.

Example 1 (non-DOG)

Analysis This is a correct description in the context of my patio even though my dog Birta is there because it describes correctly in some of the context: see, there, table-ing.

Example 2 (TOY / DOG)

Analysis I'm visiting my friend at her home when her small child points and says the "(TOY / DOG)". Each of "TOY" and "DOG" elicits a concept for me. But that's not enough to evaluate whether what she said is a correct description. I have to decide whether the concept of "TOY" as modified by the concept of "DOG" is a correct description. Though I see a stuffed toy and a dog sleeping near the table, I see where she is pointing and say "TOY / CAT".

It's not enough that each word which appears in a complex categorematic word elicits a concept we can use to evaluate the word as correct or not correct in the context. We need to evaluate whether the concept that the whole elicits applies.

Example 3 (TOY ∧ DOG)

Analysis This is correct in the context given in the last example, which we can show by noting that each of "TOY" and "DOG" are correct descriptions.

Example 4 ⌐ (TOY / DOG)

Analysis This is correct in the context given in Example 1, which we can show by noting that "TOY / DOG" is not a correct description. No toy-dog-ing.

Concepts of complex categorematic words depend on the concepts that the words that make up the complex elicit. That dependence is not a straightforward addition which can be understood by knowing the concepts that the parts elicit. A complex categorematic word has to be evaluated as a whole in a context. But, as we've seen, evaluations of compound words can be made from evaluations of the words that are compounded.

Conceptual Equivalence

15 Conceptual Equivalence and Descriptive Equivalence

When does one categorematic word elicit the same concept as another? Can that even happen? Does "DOG" elicit the same concept as "POOCH"? How can we tell? Should I look inward and try to find if they elicit the same for me and then ask you to do the same?

Perhaps we could start by asking whether one concept is contained in another. I say that the concept of "ANIMAL" is part of the concept of "DOG". You say that the concept of "DOG" is part of the concept of "ANIMAL". Who is right? What can we appeal to in order to decide? Trying to establish equivalences of concepts by looking inwards and discussing is going to be a long, contentious, and likely unfruitful project.

But in some cases we've already agreed. Recall that we said that for any categorematic words E and F,

(1) E + F is meant to elicit the same concept as F + E is meant to elicit.

So, for example,

(2) "DOG + BARK" is meant to elicit the same concept
     as "BARK + DOG" is meant to elicit.

But wait, you say, those don't elicit the same concept for me: the order of the words in them matters for how I understand the together-uses. Perhaps it does for you, but we'll say that you should adjust your concepts of these words so they do elicit the same concept. We take (1) and hence (2) to be prescriptive: this is how we should understand these words. We adopt such prescriptions in order to allow us to communicate better.

In this section I'll show how we can use the prescriptions about conceptual equivalence we've already made. This project will not be part of our talk in the flow of all but an analysis of our talk in the flow of all. It will be worthwhile if it helps us communicate and better understand our notions of concept. I say "notions" rather than "notion" for it seems unlikely that we share just one idea of concept rather than an idea of concept I have, an idea of concept you have, an idea of concept she has, an idea of concept he has. If we can establish agreements which work for all our notions of concept, we can understand concept(s) better and communicate better.

In (2) I've used quotation marks in "DOG + BARK" to indicate that I am talking about that word, not using it for describing. A choice of context is irrelevant for whether (2) is correct. But then for (1) I should have written:

"E + F" is meant to elicit the same concept as "F + E" is meant to elicit.

Here the letters are meant to stand for categorematic words. To avoid a proliferation of quotation I'm going to assume that when we use a capital letter such as E, F, or A, B, we can recognize whether it is supposed to stand for a word or for a word that has quotation marks around it. So (1) will be an acceptable way to write.

Now we can introduce an abbreviation.

Conceptual equivalence

$E \approx F \equiv_{Def}$ the categorematic word E is meant to elicit the same concept as the categorematic word F is meant to elicit

If $E \approx F$, we say that E is *conceptually equivalent to* F.

We write "$E \not\approx F$" for "E is not conceptually equivalent to F".

So now instead of (2), we'll write:

(3) "DOG + BARK" $\approx$ "BARK + DOG"

Descriptive equivalence

Given any word and context, the concept the word is meant to elicit determines — or rather allows us to determine — whether the word is a correct description. So if two words are meant to elicit the same concept, then in any context they are both correct descriptions or they are both not correct descriptions. So from (3) we have:

In any context, "DOG + BARK" is a correct description iff "BARK + DOG" is a correct description.

Let's use an abbreviation for writing about this kind of equivalence.

Descriptive equivalence

$E \equiv F \equiv_{Def}$ in any context E is a correct description iff F is a correct description

If $E \equiv F$, we say that E is *descriptively equivalent to* F.

We write "$E \not\equiv F$" for "E is not descriptively equivalent to F".

With our new notation we can state succinctly the principle relating conceptual equivalence to descriptive equivalence.

Conceptual equivalence yields descriptive equivalence For any categorematic words E and F, if $E \approx F$, then $E \equiv F$.

Example 1 "(HORSE – BROWN)" $\approx$ "(BROWN – HORSE)"

Analysis When we introduced disjoining of categorematic words we said that the order of the words in a disjoining doesn't matter for the concept the word is meant to elicit. For any categorematic words E and F, $E - F \approx F - E$. If you don't agree, take this as a prescription.

Example 2 "(ARFITO)" ≈ "(ARFITO)"

Analysis This follows from the definition of ≈. For any categorematic word E, E ≈ E.

Example 3 "(DOG + RUN)" ≈ "(DOG + DOG + RUN)"

Analysis When we introduced together-uses of categorematic words, we agreed (in our new notation) that for any categorematic word E, E + E ≈ E. So "(DOG + DOG)" ≈ "(DOG)". Hence we can replace "DOG" with "DOG + DOG" in "DOG + RUN" without changing the concept the latter is meant to elicit.

Example 4 "(TOY / (DOG – WOLF))" ≈ "(TOY / (WOLF – DOG))"

Analysis This follows because "(DOG – WOLF)" ≈ "(WOLF – DOG)", so we can replace the former with the latter in a categorematic word without changing the concept the word is meant to elicit.

In these last two examples I've used the following principle.

Substitution of conceptual equivalents If W is a categorematic word in which E appears, and E ≈ F, and Y is the result of replacing some but not necessarily all appearances of E in W with F, then W ≈ Y.

I can't justify this beyond appealing to the explanations we saw of how the concept of a complex word depends on the concepts of the words that appear in it. Combining this and the principle that conceptual equivalence yields descriptive equivalence, we have the following.

Substitution of descriptive equivalents If W is a categorematic word in which E appears, and E ≈ F, and Y is the result of replacing some but not necessarily all appearances of E in W with F, then W ≡ Y.

Example 5 "(SIBLING)" ≈ "(BROTHER – SISTER)"

Analysis How can a base word elicit the same concept as a complex word?
 The word "SIBLING" is defined or introduced as just a short way of saying "(BROTHER – SISTER)". There's nothing more to it.
 This is a conceptual equivalence that is not due to form but to stipulation.

Example 6 "(HOUSE / SIBLING)" ≈ "(HOUSE / (BROTHER – SISTER))"

Analysis This follows from the last example by substitution.

Example 7 "(non-(non-(CAT)))" ≡ "(CAT)"
         "(non-(non-(CAT)))" ≉ "(CAT)"

Analysis The first follows from how we evaluate negative categorematic words as descriptions. But "non-(non-(CAT))" and "CAT" elicit different concepts: absence of absence of cat-ing isn't the same as cat-ing. Conceptual equivalence does not follow from descriptive equivalence. But descriptive equivalence does follow here from the form of the words: for every categorematic word E, (non-(non-(E))) ≡ (E).

Example 8   "(BLACK – GREY – WHITE – CLEAR)" ≡ "(non-(COLOR))"

"(BLACK – GREY – WHITE – CLEAR)" ≉ "(non-(COLOR))"

Analysis The descriptive equivalence is not due to the form of words, nor to a stipulation, nor to a rule for how to evaluate descriptions. We have to learn that in any context "BLACK – GREY – WHITE – CLEAR" is a correct description iff "non-COLOR" is. But it seems wrong to say that these words are conceptually equivalent.

Example 9   "(DEAD)" ≢ "(non-(ALIVE))"

"(DEAD)" ≉ "(non-(ALIVE))"

Analysis In a context of rocks lying on a concrete driveway, I can correctly assert "non-ALIVE", but "DEAD" would not be a correct description, for "DEAD" can correctly describe only some of the flow of all that could previously be described with "ALIVE". Since descriptive equivalence does not hold, neither does conceptual equivalence.

Example 10   "((ARF + WALK) with (ARFITO + BARK))"
≈ "((ARFITO + BARK) with (ARF + WALK))"

Analysis We can recognize or constrain how we understand categorematic linkings, perhaps adopting a general equivalence: (E with F) ≈ (F with E).

Example 11   If "(PUP)" ≈ (POOCH)", then "(POOCH)" ≈ (PUP)".

Analysis This is not an assertion that "(PUP)" ≈ "(POOCH)" but only what follows if we assume that "(PUP)" ≈ "(POOCH)". From the definition of ≈, we have that if E ≈ F, then F ≈ E. And from the definition of descriptive equivalence, we have that if E ≡ F, then F ≡ E.

Example 12   If "(PUP)" ≈ "(POOCH)", and "((POOCH)" ≈ "(DOG)", then "(PUP)" ≈ "(DOG)".

Analysis From the definition of ≈, if E ≈ F, and F ≈ G, then E ≈ G. And similarly, from the definition of ≡, if E ≡ F, and F ≡ G, then E ≡ G.

Transitivity of conceptual equivalence   If E ≈ F, and F ≈ G, then E ≈ G.

Example 13 Taking context a patch of mud in my patio, in any context within that, "MUD" is a correct description iff "BROWN" is a correct description.

Analysis This is not due to form, or conceptual equivalence, or stipulation. It just happens that in this context these are equivalent descriptions.

Summarizing, here are ways we can make or find conceptual equivalences.

- We can agree that we'll understand the words as eliciting the same concept.
- We take as part of a definition of a kind of word that any word of that form is conceptually equivalent to any word of another specified form.
- We can derive further conceptual equivalences from conceptual equivalences we already have by using substitution.

16 Deriving Conceptual Equivalences

Deriving Conceptual Equivalences, **DCE**
The letters E, F, G, H, W, Y stand for categorematic words.

Initial schemes of equivalences due to form

1. $E/E \approx E$
2. $E + E \approx E$
3. $E + F + \ldots + G \approx H$
   where H is a together-use of $E, F, \ldots, G$ in any order, possibly with repetitions
4. $E - E \approx E$
5. $E - F - \ldots - G \approx H$
   where H is a disjoining of $E, F, \ldots, G$ in any order, possibly with repetitions

Initial particular equivalences not due to form
These are conceptual equivalences not due to form that we agree are correct.

Rules

a. If $E \approx F$, then $F \approx E$.
b. If $E \approx F$ and $F \approx G$, then $E \approx G$.
c. *Substitution*
   If E appears in W, and $E \approx F$, and Y is the result of replacing some but not necessarily all appearances of E in W with F, then $W \approx Y$.

Derivations
   A *derivation* of an equivalence $E \approx F$ is a sequence of one or more equivalences ending with $E \approx F$ in which the order matters and each of the equivalences is either an instance of one of the initial ones or follows from the preceding ones by one of the rules.

•> $(\underline{E} \approx \underline{F}) \equiv_{\text{Def}}$ there is a derivation in **DCE** of $\underline{E} \approx \underline{F}$

Each initial scheme of conceptual equivalences is correct as noted when we first presented these kinds of categorematic words. The initial particular equivalences, such as "(SIBLING)" $\approx$ "(BROTHER – SISTER)", are correct by assumption. The first two rules lead from conceptual equivalences to conceptual equivalences by the definition of conceptual equivalence. The rule of substitution leads from conceptual equivalences to conceptual equivalences, as noted in the last chapter.

Chapter 16

Hence we have:

If •> (E ≈ F), then E ≈ F.

To claim that if E ≈ F then •> (E ≈ F), even for those equivalences that are due to form, we'd need that there is nothing in the presentations in the section on categorematic words concerning the concepts of complex categorematic words that we've not taken account of with these schemes.

Example 1 "((HOUSE <u>with</u> CAR) – ((DOG + (non-BARK))))" ≈
   "(((DOG + (non-BARK))) – (HOUSE <u>with</u> CAR))"

Analysis This is an instance of initial scheme (5).

Example 2 "((DOG / RUN) + (RED / APPLE))" ≈
   "((RED / APPLE) + (DOG / RUN))"

Analysis This is an instance of initial scheme (3).

Example 3 •> "(RUN ≈ RUN)"

Analysis Here is a derivation.

   i. "(RUN / RUN)" ≈ "(RUN)"   an instance of scheme (1)
   ii. "(RUN)" ≈ "(RUN / RUN)"   rule (a) applied to (i)
   iii. "(RUN)" ≈ "(RUN)"   rule (b) applied to (ii) and (i) in that order

Note that I say "a" derivation, not "the" derivation. There may be many correct derivations of an equivalence. Here we could have started with "(RUN + RUN)" ≈ "(RUN)" as an instance of scheme (2).

Example 4 •> "(DOG + BARK)" ≈ "(DOG + BARK)"

Analysis We could go through the same steps as in the last example, replacing "RUN" with "DOG + BARK". Or we can give a scheme of derivations to show that for any categorematic word E, •> E ≈ E, and note that the example is an instance.

   i.   E / E ≈ E   scheme (1)
   ii. E ≈ E / E   rule (a) applied to (i)
   iii. E ≈ E   rule (b) applied to (ii) and (i) in that order

Example 5 For any categorematic words E, F, G, H,

   •> (E + F) – (G + H) ≈ (G + H) – (F + E)

Analysis Here is a scheme of derivations.

   i. (E + F) – (G + H) ≈ (G + H) – (E + F)   an instance of (5)
   ii. (E + F) ≈ (F + E)   an instance of (3)

iii. (G + H) − (E + F) ≈ (G + H) − (F + E)   by substitution on (i) using (ii)
iv. (E + F) − (G + H) ≈ (G + H) − (F + E)   by rule (b) on (i) and (iii)

From this example we have:

•> "((RUN + DOG) − (LAUGH + GIRL))" ≈
    "((LAUGH + GIRL) − (DOG + RUN))"

Or you could show this equivalence by tracking how these words are meant to elicit.

Example 6 not •> ((E + F) ≈ E)
Analysis We can show this by noting that "(RUN + CRY)" ≉ "(RUN)".

Example 7 not •> (E c̲ F ≈ F c̲ E)
Analysis Suppose that E c̲ F ≈ F c̲ E were derivable. An instance of it is:

    "(DOG + CHASE <u>directed towards</u> CAT)" ≈
        "(CAT <u>directed towards</u> DOG + CHASE)"

Since conceptual equivalence yields descriptive equivalence, we would have:

    "(DOG + CHASE <u>directed towards</u> CAT)" ≡
        "(CAT <u>directed towards</u> DOG + CHASE)"

But this is not correct, for the two cats might not yet be aware that the dogs are closing in on them. So (E c̲ F ≈ F c̲ E) is not derivable.

Example 8 •> "(CAT + RUN + BLACK)" ≈ "(BLACK + CAT + RUN)"
Analysis This is an instance of initial scheme (3).

Example 9 If "(SIBLING)" ≈ "(SISTER–BROTHER)" is one of the initial particular equivalences, then:

    •> "(HOUSE / SIBLING)" ≈ (HOUSE / (SISTER–BROTHER))".

Analysis This follows from the rule of substitution.

Example 10 If "(FORGET)" ≈ "non-(REMEMBER)" is one of the initial particular equivalences, then

    •> "(DOG + FORGET)" ≈ "(non-(REMEMBER) + DOG)".

Analysis Here is a derivation.

    "(FORGET)" ≈ "(non-(REMEMBER))"   an initial particular equivalence
    "(DOG + FORGET)" ≈ "(DOG + non-(REMEMBER))"   by substitution
    "(DOG + non-(REMEMBER))" ≈ "((non-(REMEMBER) + DOG)"
                                                    by initial scheme (3)
    "(DOG + FORGET)" ≈ "(non-(REMEMBER) + DOG)"   by rule (b)

If we have not agreed to take "(FORGET)" ≈ "non-(REMEMBER)" as one of the initial particular equivalences, yet you believe it should be one, then you can give an alternative system, say **DCE-alt 1**, in which it is added to the list of particular equivalences. Then we can compare consequences in these systems.

Reasoning

17 Inferences and Validity

Early morning, waking up, I listen and note that "CAT + MEOW" and "DOG + BARK" are correct descriptions . What follows from these two words being correct? Can I conclude that "DOG + CHASE <u>directed towards</u> CAT" is a correct description? I'm not sure, since I remember that "DOG <u>inside</u> FENCE" was correct when I went to bed last night. But surely "CAT + RUN" is correct.

What we say follows from noting that some word or words are correct descriptions depends so much on our experience, on what we know about the world, and what we think will continue. So it seems that any analysis of what we're justified in saying follows from a word or words being correct descriptions will depend on our personal lives and the assumptions we make in our language-culture. To give an analysis of that is more than we can do here, not least because you and I are not fully immersed in a culture that depends on experiencing the world as the flow of all. And even if we were, we would at best be able to describe what we are more or less justified in concluding from "DOG + BARK" and "CAT + MEOW" in this context.

What we can conclude with confidence is that if "DOG + BARK" is a correct description, then "DOG" and "BARK" are, too. If "DOG <u>inside</u> FENCE" was a correct description last night, then so was "DOG" and "FENCE" and "DOG ∧ FENCE". If "DOG + CHASE <u>directed towards</u> CAT" is correct, then "DOG + CHASE" would be, too. So if I get up and look out the window and see that "¬ CHASE" is correct, then I can conclude that "¬ (DOG + CHASE <u>directed towards</u> CAT)" is correct. It's not because of how we understand "DOG" and "FENCE" that we can conclude from "DOG <u>inside</u> FENCE" having been a correct description so was "DOG ∧ FENCE" but because of the forms of the words, knowing how they are meant to be evaluated.

But it's not just forms of words that ensure we can conclude with certainty. Since the concept elicited by "SIBLING" is the same as the concept elicited by "BROTHER–SISTER", from "HOUSE / SIBLING" being a correct description, we can conclude that "HOUSE / (BROTHER – SISTER)" is, too.

To investigate how we can conclude, let's begin with some definitions.

Inferences An *inference* is two or more words, one of which is designated the *conclusion* and the others the *premises*, which is intended by the person who sets it out as either showing that the conclusion follows from the premises or investigating whether that is the case. The order of the premises does not matter.

We indicate that we are considering an inference with premises A, B, . . . and conclusion C by writing or saying: A, B, . . . *therefore* C .

Valid inferences An inference is *valid* means that in any context in which each of the premises is a correct descriptions, so is the conclusion. If an inference is not valid, it is *invalid*. We say that the conclusion of a valid inference *follows from* the premises; it is a *consequence* of the premises.

Valid words A word is *valid* means that in any context it is a correct description. If it is not valid, it is *invalid*.

Example 1 (DOG + BARK + CHASE) therefore (CAT)

Analysis This is an inference, where "therefore" indicates that someone (me in this case) has put it forward. It's not valid, since the premise is a correct description of the field near my home where my dog Arfito is chasing a gopher with no cat in sight or smell.

Example 2 (DOG inside FENCE) therefore (DOG)

Analysis This is a valid inference: "DOG" is a correct description in any context in which "DOG inside FENCE" is a correct description, as we know from how we evaluate the latter.

Example 3 (DOG) therefore (DOG inside FENCE)

Analysis This is not a valid inference. As I am writing now, "DOG" is a correct description of the area around my house, but "(DOG inside FENCE)" is not— Arfito and his doggy friend are lying in the shade under the tree.

Example 4 (DOG) ∨ ¬ (DOG)

Analysis This is valid. In any context there is dog-ing or there is complete absence of dog-ing.

Example 5 (CAT) ∨ ¬ (DOG)

Analysis This is not valid. As I am writing now, "¬ (DOG)" is not a correct description of the area around my house because Arfito-ing is there, and also "CAT" is not correct.

We can talk of forms of inferences by using schemes of words.

Schemes of inferences A *scheme of inferences* is two or more schemes of words one of which is designated the *conclusion* scheme and the others *premise* schemes.

If all compatible instances of a scheme of inferences are valid, the scheme is *valid*. Otherwise it is *invalid*.

An inference that is a compatible instance of a scheme of inferences has the *form* of that scheme if
- distinct upper-case letters are replaced by distinct words and
- distinct lower-case letters are replaced by distinct categorematic linkings.

Example 6 (F + G + H) therefore E

Analysis This is a form of an inference. Example 1 is an instance, so it is not valid.

Example 7 F therefore E

Analysis This is a form of an inference, of which Example 1 is also an instance.

Example 8 ¬ (E c̲ G) ∧ ¬ (F d̲ H) therefore ¬ ((E c̲ G) – (F d̲ H))

Analysis This is a scheme of valid inferences. The following has the form of it.

 ¬ (CAR near HOUSE) ∧ ¬ (WIND directed towards TREE) therefore

 ¬ ((CAR near HOUSE)) – (WIND directed towards TREE))

Here is a compatible instantiation of the scheme that does not have the form of the example.

 ¬ (CAR near CAR) ∧ ¬ (CAR near CAR) therefore

 ¬ ((CAR near CAR)) – (CAR near CAR))

That's because distinct letters are not replaced by distinct words.

18 Scenarios

What do we mean by "any context"?

We can specify a context any way we can draw someone's attention to some of the flow of all: pointing, touching, smelling, feeling, tasting, describing in words, a picture, ... Recall the picture I took in my corral.

In this context, "SHEEP" is a correct description. In some of the context, "SHEEP" correctly describes, though in some of the context it does not:

No more than I or you or anyone can specify all contexts, we cannot specify all contexts within the context depicted in the first picture of my corral. When we talk of all contexts, we have to mean all contexts we are willing and able to draw someone's attention to. There is not a "reality" of all the contexts in my corral any more than there is a reality of all waters in the water in my bathtub.

Since we cannot talk of all contexts except as motivation, we specify a general context to consider, then we specify contexts within that as the ones we'll pay attention to. We don't list "them". We give ways we agree will lead us to pay attention together. We can take as general context my corral as pictured in the first photo above. Within that general context, we can understand "any context" to be what we can circumscribe through drawing, or computer trimming, or outlining with a pencil or pen, as in the second picture. That is still open-ended. But I can tell if you've specified a context readily enough.

We start with a stock of categorematic words and linkings, which we can add to as we wish. The concepts which these categorematic words are meant to elicit and our understandings of the categorematic linkings do not depend on what method of specifying contexts we are considering. When we talk about the ancient Gaels, "DOG" is meant to elicit what it does for us talking of my ranch. When we talk of weather conditions in the Gila National Forest in New Mexico, "FIRE" is meant to elicit what it does for us in talking of my neighbor burning his trash. When we use "((MOTHER with BABY) + RUN) from EXPLODE" in the context of dropping an atomic bomb on Hiroshima, we understand "from" as we do in describing a gopher running from Arfito along the irrigation canal near where I live.

So each categorematic word we use, base or complex, elicits a concept for us. Then if you draw my attention to a context, I can decide whether the concept applies. That is, I can decide whether the word is a correct description in that context. Or at least I hope I can. You might disagree. It might not be obvious: there is the imprecision of how we specify a context and the difference in how we understand words and categorematic linkings. Worse, thinking of motives for reasoning, it's not always obvious what categorematic words are correct descriptions.

- We want to check that we haven't made a mistake.

    Is "MOLE" or "GOPHER" a correct description in a field
    near where I live?

- We want to plan for the future.

    What will be the consequences if "FIRE" continues to be a correct
    description in the Gila National Forest in New Mexico next week?

- We want to know more about the past.

    We know so little about the ancient Gaels. So we ask what follows
    from what we do know.

- We want to consider ways the world could have been in order to guide
  our actions now.

    What would have followed if President Truman had not ordered
    that Hiroshima be destroyed by an atomic bomb?

Let's set up ways we can compare our differences in evaluating which categorematic words are correct in which context.

Scenarios A *scenario* is:
- a general context we agree on;
- ways we agree can lead us to pay attention together to contexts within the general context;
- evaluations as needed of categorematic words as correct or incorrect descriptions for any context we pay attention to within the general context, including the general context itself.

Evaluations of compound words then follow.

What if we want to reason about what would follow if we assume that in the area around where I live there are pigs that can fly? In this imagined scenario "PIG" can't elicit the same concept as when talking of my friend's farm where he raises a few pigs. Is "PIG + MAMMAL" correct or is "PIG + BIRD"? Let's avoid specifying a scenario where we can't use our categorematic words and categorematic linkings with our usual understandings.[9] To reason about flying pigs we will have to make a new word, say "FPIG", and agree on a concept it elicits for pigs that can fly. Good luck.

Can't we be more precise, more rigid, so that there are no open-ends in setting up a scenario? I don't see how. And if you think this is hard, try to set up a scenario for when I'm with my friend and I sniff and say "SMOKE". We never describe all. We point in whatever way we can to help the other person pay attention as we do, at least enough for us to talk together. A "real" scenario, complete and fixed, there for us to recognize and not establish, is a fairy-land dream.

Note that we, people, are involved in every step of setting out a scenario and hence what we mean by "any context". I do not see how a human-independent analysis of reasoning in the world as the flow of all could be made.

Valid inferences in a scenario *An inference is valid in a scenario* means that in any context within the general context of the scenario in which the premises are correct descriptions, the conclusion is a correct description.

Valid words in a scenario *A word is valid in a scenario* means that it is a correct description in any context within the general context of the scenario.

Since scenarios are meant to make clear what we mean by "every context", we have the following.

---

[9] This problem isn't peculiar to talk about the world as the flow of all. We have no clear idea how to reason about such an example in talk of the world as made up of things. See my "Conditionals".

Chapter 18

Valid inferences and valid words

An inference is valid iff it is valid in every scenario.

A word is valid iff it is valid in every scenario.

We adopt the following notations.

R, S, T, and other bold-face capital letters stand for scenarios.

$A, B, \ldots \vDash_S C$ the inference $A, B, \ldots$ *therefore* C is valid in scenario **S**

$A, B, \ldots \vDash C$ the inference $A, B, \ldots$ *therefore* C is valid

$\vDash_S A$ the word A is valid in scenario **S**

$\vDash A$ the word A is valid

We write $\nvDash$ for "is not valid" and $\nvDash_S$ for "is not valid in scenario **S**".

The notation for word validity is compatible with that for inference validity since a word is valid iff it is a consequence of no premises at all.

Recall from Chapter 15, for any categorematic words E and F,

$E \approx F \equiv_{Def}$ E is meant to elicit the same concept as F is meant to elicit

Substitution

If E appears in W, and $E \approx F$, and Y is the result of replacing some but not necessarily all appearances of E in W with F, then $W \approx Y$.

$E \equiv F \equiv_{Def}$ for any context, E is correct iff F is correct

If $E \approx F$, then $E \equiv F$.

And in our new notation,

If $E \equiv F$, then $E \vDash F$ and $F \vDash E$.

19 Examples of Evaluating in Scenarios

When I present a general context with a photo, unless noted otherwise contexts within it are what we can circumscribe through drawing, or computer trimming, or outlining with a pencil or pen, or pointing with an index finger.

Example 1 Take as general context for a scenario **G** what is depicted in this photo that I took in my bedroom on March 16, 2024, at 10:17 p.m.

BLACK

Analysis This is a correct description in the general context. Moreover, it is a correct description in any context within that — we don't have to survey ways of trimming the picture. So "BLACK" is valid in this scenario: $\vDash_{\mathbf{G}} (\text{BLACK})$.

But $\nvDash (\text{BLACK})$, for "BLACK" fails to be a correct description in the context within the general context of my corral depicted in the second picture on p. 69.

Could any base categorematic word be valid? If one were, it could not be used to distinguish in the flow of all, just as "BLACK" cannot be used to distinguish in Example 1. And if a word cannot be incorrect in any context, there can be no understanding.[10] Or at least it seemed so to me until I thought of "TIME". But perhaps "TIME" is not valid, since there is no before and after in the context of my corral depicted on p. 69. But then I thought of "SPACE". Isn't "SPACE" or the restricted word "LOCATION" a correct description in every context? To say no is to allow for scenarios in which there is no location, and I can't even imagine that much less how we would evaluate words in such a scenario. Yet if we take "SPACE" to be valid, we cannot use it to describe in the flow of all. This location or that location that we might have a word for that which we could use in descriptions, but not "SPACE".

---

[10] However, a word that is incorrect in every context can be meaningful, for example PEGASUS.

Example 2 For scenario **M** with general context a patch of mud in my yard,

⊨_{**M**} (MUD)

Analysis This seems right: every part of mud-ing is mud-ing.

But what if there's a pebble in that patch of mud? Can't we specify a context in which "PEBBLE" is correct and "MUD" is not? This is not an issue about what what is mud-ing and how mud-ing can be divided. To accept the example is to place a restriction on what we will take as context within the general context.

Note that we can effect the same restriction on what counts as context within the general context by assuming that "¬ (non-MUD)" is correct in **M**.

"¬ (non-MUD)" is a correct description in the general context iff

"(non-MUD)" is not a correct description in the general context iff

"MUD" is a correct description in every context within the general context

That is, "¬ (non-MUD)" is a correct description in **M** iff ⊨_{**M**} (MUD). Generally:

For any scenario **S** and any categorematic word E,

¬ (non-E) is a correct description in **S** iff ⊨_{**S**} E.

Stipulating that ¬ (non-E) is a correct description in the scenario ensures that we are considering only contexts in which E is correct.

Example 3 Talking about chicken-ing

Analysis Suppose we're talking about my corral and adopt a scenario **C** with general context as in the top photo on p. 69. We can stipulate that we'll consider only contexts in which "CHICKEN" is correct by requiring that "¬ (non-CHICKEN)" is a correct description in it. That would rule out as a context in the scenario what is pictured below.

What is a correct description in a scenario depends on what contexts we are considering. We can specify those by using descriptions, including negative ones. This still relies on our thing-talk or some other pointing to establish the general context.

Example 4 SHEEP − (non-(SHEEP))

Analysis Is this a correct description in the scenario **C** of my corral (top p. 69)?

Did you look to check? You needn't. We can conclude it's correct just by knowing how to evaluate it: locally, there, either sheep-ing or absence of sheep-ing. For any categorematic word E, ⊨ (E − (non-E)).

A complex categorematic word can be valid due to its form.

Example 5   ¬ (DOG + CAT)

Analysis "DOG + CAT" is never a correct description because in any context dog-ing can be (conceptually) spatially separated from cat-ing, and we've agreed to understand words the same in every scenario. So "¬ (DOG + CAT)" is a correct description in any context. That is, for every scenario S, ⊨$_S$ ¬ (DOG + CAT), and hence ⊨ ¬ (DOG + CAT). This is a word that is valid due to the concepts the words in it elicit, not due to its form, for "¬ (DOG + BARK)" is not correct now as I write.

Example 6   In scenario **W** with general context what can be seen from my office window,

¬ (CAR) ∧ ¬ (non-CAR)

Analysis   "¬ (CAR) ∧ ¬ (non-CAR)" is a correct description in a context iff

iff   "¬ (CAR)" is correct and "¬¬ (non-CAR)" is correct

iff   in none of the context is "CAR" correct
and in none of the context is "non-CAR" correct

iff   in none of the context is "CAR" correct
and in some of the context "CAR" is correct

This cannot be. We've discovered: ⊨$_W$ ¬ (¬ (CAR) ∧ ¬ (non-CAR)).

This analysis applies in any scenario and for any categorematic word in place of "CAR". That is, ⊨ ¬ (¬ (E) ∧ ¬ (non-E)).

Example 7   ¬ (SHEEP ∧ (non-SHEEP))

Analysis This is not valid. In the context of my corral (top p. 69), "SHEEP" is correct (look, there, sheep-ing) and also "non-SHEEP" is correct (look, in the second picture—no sheep-ing). So ⊭ ¬ (E ∧ (non-E)).

Example 8   ¬ (SHEEP ∧ ¬ (SHEEP))

Analysis This is valid: for any scenario, either there is sheep-ing in some of the general context, or there is no sheep-ing in the general context. For any categorematic word E, ⊨ ¬ (E ∧ ¬ E).

Example 9   ¬ (((RUN ∧ SLEEP) ∧ RAIN) ∧ ¬ (((RUN ∧ SLEEP) ∧ RAIN))

Analysis This is getting complicated. We can make better sense of it if we look at its form: ¬ (((E ∧ F) ∧ G) ∧ ¬ (((E ∧ F) ∧ G)). Simplifying further, we have the form ¬ (A ∧ ¬ A). We just saw that this is valid when E is a categorematic

76 Chapter 19

word. And it's valid when A is a compound word: we can't have that both A is a correct description and A is not a correct description.

Example 10 For the scenario **C** of my corral (top p. 69),

DONKEY $\vDash_C$ (BROWN – WHITE – BLACK)

Analysis Just look at the picture. But looking at the context within **C** depicted in the second picture on p. 69, we can see,

(BROWN – WHITE – BLACK) $\nvDash_C$ DONKEY

Example 11 For the scenario **C** of my corral (p. 69),

DONKEY $\vDash_C$ (BROWN – WHITE – BLACK – GREEN)

Analysis It's enough to consider the conditions for these words to be correct descriptions to note that we have:

(BROWN – WHITE – BLACK) $\vDash$ (BROWN – WHITE – BLACK – GREEN)

So we have:

(BROWN – WHITE – BLACK) $\vDash_C$ (BROWN – WHITE – BLACK – GREEN)

Combining Example 10 and this, we get that the example is correct. Generalizing, we have the following.

Transitivity of validity For any scenario **S**, if $A \vDash_S B$ and $B \vDash_S C$, then $A \vDash_S C$.
  If $A \vDash B$ and $B \vDash C$, then $A \vDash C$.

Example 12 Take as scenario **Q** with general context what is depicted in this photo of my patio in the snow.

WHITE $\vDash_Q$ (SNOW – SKY)

Analysis But $F \nvDash (G - H)$, as you can show with an example.

Example 13 For the scenario **Q** of the last example,

DOG $\vDash_Q$ SNOW

Analysis This is correct because "DOG" is not a correct description in the general context.

Example 14 For the scenario **Q**,

$$(SNOW-DOG) \nvDash_Q DOG$$

Analysis The premise is a correct description in **Q**, but the conclusion isn't. Hence, $(F-G) \nvDash G$.

Example 15 For the scenario **Q**,

$$SNOW \vDash_Q (SNOW-DOG)$$

Analysis We don't need to inspect contexts in **Q**. Just consider the conditions for a description to be correct in a scenario and the conditions for validity. For any categorematic words E and F, $E \vDash (E-F)$.

Example 16 $(TOY/DOG) \nvDash DOG$.

Analysis Take as general context what is depicted in the photo of Ralph in the front matter of this book. So $(E/F) \nvDash F$.

Example 17 $DOG \vDash DOG$

Analysis This is correct by the definition of valid inference. Generally, for any word A, categorematic or compound $A \vDash A$.

Example 18 For the scenario **W** of the world as we know it now, supposing that we've agreed on how we'll specify contexts within that,

If $(DOG \& HUMAN) \vDash_W LOVE$ and $LOVE \vDash_W HAPPY$,

then $(DOG \& HUMAN) \vDash_W HAPPY$.

Analysis Did you try to think this through worrying about the concepts elicited by the words? It follows by the transitivity of validity.

Example 19 $(DOG-CAT) \nvDash (DOG + CAT)$

Analysis This is because "(DOG–CAT)" can be a correct description in a context, such as my back yard, but as we noted in Example 5, "(DOG + CAT)" is not a correct description in any context. We invoke the concepts of the words in the inference to show this is invalid.

Example 20 $(DOG-CAT) \vDash (CAT-DOG)$

Analysis "(DOG–CAT)" is meant to elicit the same concept as "(CAT–DOG)". Since the concept of a word determines whether it is a correct description in a context, in any context if "(DOG–CAT)" is a correct description, so is "(CAT–DOG)". And we also have:

$$(CAT-DOG) \vDash (DOG-CAT)$$

This example is correct because of the form of the words in it, since for any categorematic words E and F, E − F is meant to elicit the same concept as F − E. That is, E ≈ F. And hence E ≡ F. And hence E ⊨ F and F ⊨ E.

Example 21   ⊨ (DOG − CAT) ⊃ (CAT − DOG)

Analysis   Recall that "(DOG − CAT) ⊃ (CAT − DOG)" is a correct description in a context iff if "(DOG − CAT)" is a correct description in that context iff "(CAT − DOG)" is correct, which is what we saw in the last example.

Example 22   For scenario **C** of my corral as depicted at the top of p. 69,

SHEEP ⊨$_C$ (BROWN − BLACK − WHITE)

Analysis   Look at the picture. In any context in **C** in which "SHEEP" is a correct description, so is "(BROWN − BLACK − WHITE)". So it follows that:

⊨$_C$ (SHEEP) ⊃ (BROWN − BLACK − WHITE)

Generally we have the following.

Validity of inferences reduced to validity of words

A ⊨ B   iff   ⊨ A ⊃ B

A, ..., B, C ⊨ D   iff   A, ..., B ⊨ (C ⊃ D)

Example 23   (TOY / (DOG − CAT)) ⊨ (TOY / (CAT − DOG))

Analysis   Since "(CAT − DOG)" ≈ "(DOG − CAT)", we have by substitution "TOY / (DOG − CAT)" ≈ "TOY / (CAT − DOG)", and so the example follows.

The example is correct due to the form of the words. For any categorematic words E, F, and K, if E ≈ F, then K / F ≡ K / E, and hence K / F ⊨ K / E.

Example 24   (HOUSE / SIBLING) ⊨ (HOUSE / (BROTHER − SISTER))

Analysis   In Example 5 of Chapter 15 we said,

"SIBLING" ≈ "(BROTHER − SISTER)"

So reasoning as in the last example, the example is valid. But that's not due to the forms of the words.

Example 25   Not many people in New Mexico are aware that jackals are classified as canines. So we could stipulate for a scenario with general context the state of New Mexico this year,

"(CANINE)" ≈ "(DOG − FOX − COYOTE − WOLF)"

Analysis   To allow conceptual equivalences relative to a scenario would amount to changing how we'll understand words for the scenario. But then we'd have the problem of how to discern whether a word is a correct description in the general context of the scenario. If we were to assume that "DOG" ≈ "CAT", is "DOG" a correct description in a scenario with general context the area in front of my home where Arfito is sleeping?

Our agreement that we understand categorematic words the same in every context precludes making a specification of a conceptual equivalence for just one or several scenarios.

Reviewing what we've seen in this chapter, here are ways we can show that an inference or a word is valid or invalid.

1. We can cite general considerations to show that an inference is valid, such as: from $A \wedge B$ and $\neg A$, we can conclude B.
   Or we can cite general considerations to show that a word is valid, such as $\neg (A \wedge \neg A)$.

2. We can specify a scenario, invoking general observations about what we "see" there to claim that in every context in which the premises are correct the conclusion is too.
   Or we can "see" that in every context in the scenario the word is correct and hence the word is valid in the scenario.

3. We can specify a scenario in which the premises are correct and conclusion is not correct to show that the inference is not valid.
   Or we can specify a scenario in which it is "clear" that a word is not correct to show that the word is not valid.

4. We can rely on the concepts elicited by the word(s) to show that an inference is not valid or that a word is not valid.

Aside: How hard it is to specify scenarios
Here is what Joan Tough says in *The Development of Meaning*:

> When we recall past experience there is no doubt that we are dependent for the most part on language as the means of communicating our memories to others. Some reference, or some question in the present situation, leads us to inspect with 'an inward eye' recalled events or situations. Sometimes, perhaps, as we do this we are conscious that we are calling up images of those events and trying to inspect them almost as though they were scenes in the present so that we may report on them. Sometimes we are conscious that we cannot reproduce the scene inwardly and so say we just cannot remember. At other times, perhaps, we feel that we have images of the events or situation we want to communicate but that matching them with verbal accounts is too difficult. Often we bring gesture, or role play to our aid, or draw a diagram, picture or map, or demonstrate through the use of other materials, or use similes and analogies to help us make our meaning clear. Often, too, we appeal to the other to use his own past experience of similar situations: 'You know what I'm talking about, don't you?'
>   But frequently, also, we are not aware that we are using visual or kinesthetic imagery as a basis for recall. If images are there they are glimpsed momentarily; we are more conscious of the inner verbalisations that we use as we consider what we can say.
>   pp. 111–112

20 A System for Deriving Valid Words and Valid Inferences, IXN

E, F, G, H, K, L stand for categorematic words.
A, B, C, D stand for any words, categorematic or compound.

Initial schemes of words

a. (E/F) ⊃ E

b. (E/E) ⊃ E

c. E ⊃ (E/E)

d. (E + F + ... + H) ⊃ K
    where K is one of E, F, ... , H

e. (E + F + ... + H) ⊃ L
    where L is a together-use of some but not necessarily all
    of E, F, ... , H, in any order, possibly more than once

f. L ⊃ (E + F + ... + H)
    where L is a together-use in which each of E, F, ... , H,
    appears in any order, possibly more than once

g. (E c̲ F) ⊃ E

h. (E c̲ F) ⊃ F

i. K ⊃ (E − F − ... − H)
    where K is one of E, F, ... , H

j. L ⊃ (E − F − ... − H)
    where L is a disjoining of some but not necessarily all of
    E, F, ... , H, in any order, possibly more than once

k. (E − F − ... − H) ⊃ L
    where L is a disjoining in which each of E, F, ... , H appears,
    in any order, possibly more than once

l. (E − E) ⊃ E

m. (non-(non-E)) ⊃ E

n. E ⊃ (non-(non-E))

o. E − (non-E)

p. ⌐E ⊃ non-E

q. (E − F) ⊃ (E ∨ F)

r. $(E \lor F) \supset (E - F)$

s. $\neg(\neg E \land \neg(\text{non-E}))$

Compound schemes

1. $B \supset (A \supset B)$
2. $(A \supset (B \supset C)) \supset ((A \supset B) \supset (A \supset C))$
3. $(A \land B) \supset A$
4. $(A \land B) \supset B$
5. $A \supset (B \supset (A \land B))$
6. $\neg A \supset (A \supset B)$
7. $(A \supset B) \supset ((\neg A \supset B) \supset B)$

Derivations of words

A derivation of a word is a sequence of one or more words ending with that word in which the order matters and each of the words in the sequence:

- is an instance of one of the initial schemes (a)–(s) or (1)–(7).
- is an instance of $(E \supset F)$ where $E \approx F$ is derivable in the system for deriving conceptual equivalences **DCE** of Chapter 16.
- follows from one or more of the preceding words by the rule:
  From A and $(A \supset B)$, conclude B.

We call this system for deriving valid words **IXN**. We write:

$\vdash A \equiv_{\text{Def}}$ A is derivable

$\nvdash A \equiv_{\text{Def}}$ A is not derivable

Derivable words are valid If $\vdash A$, then $\vDash A$.

I'll sketch how we can show this.

The initial schemes are valid

- The initial schemes (a)–(o) were shown to be valid in the section on categorematic words.
- Scheme (p) was noted to be valid on p. 41.
- Schemes (q) and (r) were noted to be valid on p. 43.
- Scheme (s) was noted to be valid on p. 75.
- The compound word schemes (1)–(7) can be shown to be valid by

recalling from p. 44 of Chapter 12 that for any words A and B, (A ⊃ B) is a correct description in a context is equivalent to if A is a correct description, then so is B.

Conceptual equivalence yields valid inference
- If E ≈ F is derivable in **DCE**, then E ⊨ F. Hence ⊨ E ⊃ F.

The rule leads from valid words to valid words
If ⊨ A and ⊨ A ⊃ B, then ⊨ B.

Hence for any derivation, each word in the sequences is valid. So in particular, the final word in the derivation is valid.

I have no reason to think that for every A, if ⊨ A then ⊢ A. The schemes (q)–(s) are ones I just happened to think of for examples. However, in an aside at the end of this chapter I explain how we can show the following.

Derivability of valid compound word schemes Every valid compound word scheme is derivable from the initial schemes (1)–(7).

Hence, for any compound word scheme A, if ⊨ A then ⊢ A. So for any compound word scheme we have ⊨ A iff ⊢ A. So we can use the following.

(‡) If A is an instantiation of a valid compound word scheme, then we can insert it in a derivation, understanding that a derivation of A is to be inserted there.

Example 1 ⊢ (DOG ⊃ DOG)
Analysis Here is a derivation of ⊢ A ⊃ A, from which the example follows.

(i)	A ⊃ ((A ⊃ A) ⊃ A)	by (1)
(ii)	A ⊃ (A ⊃ A)	by (2)
(iii)	A ⊃ ((A ⊃ A) ⊃ A)) ⊃ ((A ⊃ ((A ⊃ A)) ⊃ (A ⊃ A))	by (2)
(iv)	(A ⊃ (A ⊃ A)) ⊃ (A ⊃ A)	rule applied to (i) and (iii)
(v)	(A ⊃ A)	rule applied to (ii) and (iv)

Alternatively, we could show the example by noting that E ≈ E is derivable in **DCE** (Example 4, Chapter 16).

Example 2 ⊢ (DOG ∧ CAT) ⊃ (CAT ∧ DOG)
Analysis Since (A ∧ B) ⊃ (B ∧ A) is a valid compound word scheme, we have ⊢ (A ∧ B) ⊃ (B ∧ A). The example is an instance of this.

Example 3 ⊬ (SNOW − DOG) ⊃ DOG

Analysis If ⊢ (SNOW – DOG) ⊃ DOG, then ⊨ (SNOW – DOG) ⊃ DOG. In Example 14 of Chapter 19 we saw that (SNOW – DOG) ⊭ DOG. Hence by validity of inferences reduced to validity of words, ⊭ (SNOW – DOG) ⊃ DOG. Since derivability implies validity, ⊬ (SNOW – DOG) ⊃ DOG.

Example 4   ⊢ E ⊃ (E + E)

Analysis From **DCE** we have (E + E) ≈ E. Hence, by the definition of derivation, ⊢ E ⊃ (E + E).

Example 5   ⊢ (¬¬ CAT) ⊃ CAT

Analysis This follows because (¬¬ A) ⊃ A is a valid compound word form and hence ⊢ (¬¬ A) ⊃ A.

Example 6   ⊢ ¬ DOG ⊃ ¬ (DOG <u>chase</u> CHICKEN)

Analysis Here is a derivation of ¬ E ⊃ ¬ (E c̲ F) for any categorematic words E, F and categorematic linking c̲.

(i)	(E c̲ F) ⊃ E	by initial scheme (g)
(ii)	(A ⊃ B) ⊃ (¬ B ⊃ ¬ A)	by (‡)
(iii)	((E c̲ F) ⊃ E) ⊃ (¬ E ⊃ ¬ (E c̲ F))	an instantiation of (i)
(iv)	¬ E ⊃ ¬ (E c̲ F)	the rule applied to (i) and (iii)

Example 7   ⊢ (HOUSE / (DOG + SLEEP)) ⊃ (HOUSE / (SLEEP + DOG))

Analysis Here is a derivation of ⊢ E / (F + G) ⊃ E / (G + F) for any categorematic words E, F, and G, of which the example is an instance.

F + G ≈ G + F	an initial equivalence of **DCE**
E / (F + G) ≈ E / (G + F)	substitution in **DCE**

Hence we have the single-step derivation;

   E / (F + G) ⊃ E / (G + F)

Generally, if •> E ≈ F in **DCE**, then for any categorematic word K, ⊢ K / E ⊃ K / F.

Example 8   ⊢ DOOR + (HOUSE / (DOG + SLEEP)) ⊃
               DOOR + (HOUSE / (SLEEP + DOG))

Analysis We just noted that in **DCE**, E / (F + G) ≈ E / (G + F). Hence in **DCE** by substitution we have: H + (E / (F + G)) ≈ H + (E / (G + F)). Hence we have the single-step derivation:

   H + (E / (F + G)) ⊃ H + (E / (G + F))

Deriving valid inferences

Derivation of an inference An inference A, B, C, ... *therefore* D is derivable in **IXN** means that there is a derivation of D in **IXN** as supplemented by A, B, C, ... That is, the following clause is added to the definition of "derivation":

- is one of A, B, C, ...

If there is such a derivation, we write:

A, B, C, ... ⊢ D

We write ⊬ for "is not derivable".

I will leave to you to show the following. The second part follows because validity of inferences can be reduced to validity of words (p. 78).

Derivable inferences are valid

If A, B, C, ... ⊢ D, then A, B, C, ... ⊨ D.

Derivability of inferences reduced to derivability of words

A ⊢ B iff ⊢ A ⊃ B

A, ..., B, C ⊢ D iff A, ..., B ⊢ (C ⊃ D)

Given an inference with more than one premise we can reduce the premises one by one until we need investigate only whether a word is valid. Note that we now have that for any categorematic words E and F,

E ≡ F iff ⊨ (E ⊃ F) ∧ (F ⊃ E)

Example 9 (HORSE ∧ COW) ⊢ COW

Analysis This follows because ⊢ (A ∧ B) ⊃ B via initial scheme (4).

Example 10 DOG, ¬ DOG ⊢ CAT

Analysis By initial scheme (6), ⊢ ¬ DOG ⊃ (DOG ⊃ CAT). Hence, ¬ DOG ⊢ (DOG ⊃ CAT). Hence, ¬ DOG, DOG ⊢ CAT. But the order of the premises does not matter. So DOG, ¬ DOG ⊢ CAT.

For any word A, we have A, ¬ A ⊢ A. It might seem that this is worthless for reasoning, since we know that both A and ¬ A cannot both be correct descriptions in a context. But reasoning with someone we might lead him or her to assert both A and ¬ A as correct descriptions in a context, and then we can show that he or she is wrong by showing that some word we know he or she won't accept as correct would then be a correct description.

Example 11   ¬¬ E ⊢ non-(non-E)

Analysis   In Example 5 we noted that ⊢ (¬¬ E) ⊃ E. So ¬¬ E ⊢ E. By initial scheme (n), ⊢ E ⊃ non-(non-E). So E ⊢ non-(non-E). So ¬¬ E ⊢ non-(non-E) using the following, which I will let you establish.

Transitivity of derivability   If A ⊢ B and B ⊢ C, then A ⊢ C.

Deriving words and inferences valid in a scenario

Recall that in Example 12 of Chapter 19 we established scenario **Q** with a picture of my patio in the snow.

We can see that "SNOW" and "SKY" are correct descriptions. Starting with these, we can derive other correct descriptions by allowing "SNOW" and "SKY" to be used as premises in a derivation. For example,

(i)	SNOW	assumption
(ii)	SKY	assumption
(iii)	SNOW ⊃ (SKY ⊃ (SNOW∧ SKY))	by initial scheme (5)
(iv)	(SKY ⊃ (SNOW∧ SKY))	by rule (*c*) from (i) and (iii)
(v)	(SNOW∧ SKY)	by rule (*c*) from (ii) and (iv)

Extending our methods?

Suppose we wish to find out what would follow if we assume some word or inference is correct in all scenarios? Should we allow for derivations in **IXN** from that word or inference and see what we can derive?

Besides the notational difficulties, this would mistake the role of our base system **IXN**. That system is meant to incorporate our methods for deriving valid words and valid inferences. If we think we should add to it, we can, and then we'd have an augmented system. We already have motive for that. From Example 8 of Chapter 15 we have both:

(*)   (BLACK – GREY – WHITE – CLEAR) ⊃ non-COLOR

non-COLOR ⊃ (BLACK – GREY – WHITE – CLEAR)

86   *Chapter 20*

We can add these to **IXN** and get a new system, which we might call **IXN+**, reckoning that to be a better basic system.

Derivations and reasoning
What is the point of codifying how to derive valid words and valid inferences via derivations? We already have methods for evaluating whether a description is good, and using scenarios we can use those to evaluate whether one description (word) follows from one or more others.

The formal system allows us another way to isolate our assumptions about describing in the flow of all.. If you accept these initial words and inferences as valid, and you accept that the derivations lead from valid words and inferences to a valid word or inference, then we can reason together using the notion of validity, regardless of what idea of correct description you have that might be different from what we have been using here.

If in adopting some descriptions as correct not based on form, such as (*), we might disagree. In that case, using the system here we can see the consequences of adopting a particular description as correct.

Aside: Any word valid due to its form as a compound word can be derived
In Chapter II of *Propositional Logics* I present an axiom system for classical propositional logic in the language of ¬ and → using the single rule: if A and A → B, then B. I give a constructive proof that every valid formula can be derived in that system. Then I present an axiom system for classical propositional logic in the language of ¬ and ∧ to which that proof can be adapted by reading ⊃ for → . If we read "categorematic word" for "atomic proposition", "correct description" for "true", "not correct description" for "false", and "scenario" for "model", that proof can apply here. As the proof is constructive, it seems that we could formulate it for talk in the world as the flow of all. As part of that proof, we get what is called "the syntactic deduction theorem", which here is the derivability of inferences reduced to derivability of words.

Much of the work on axiomatizations of propositional logics in that book is to deal with axiom systems that allow inferences with infinitely many premises, an assumption that doesn't make sense in talk of the world as the flow of all.

Talk of Context
in the Flow of All

21 Words for Contexts

Talk of context in the flow of all
To evaluate a categorematic word we must indicate, point in some way to a context in which it is meant as correct or incorrect. Pointing is outside our talk in the flow of all. However, we can make words to stand for our pointing, to describe contexts. Doing so we will be able to bring some of how we evaluate words into our talk in the flow of all.

Context words
We can make new words to stand for establishing context. For example, we can make a word "PTO" to stand for establishing as context my patio this morning. Here are several such words to start our discussion.

word	stands for context
PTO	the patio of Arf's ranch this morning
CRL	the corral at Arf's ranch last night
CORL	the corral at Arf's ranch
SHD	the shed in the corral at Arf's ranch
DGS	Arf's ranch Dogshine
SCR	Socorro County, New Mexico
NZ	New Zealand

It might seem that our words describe context via talk of time and location. But "DGS" is not tied to a specific time and location: I added to my ranch over the years and separated off some of it, too. Nor is "NZ" meant to pick out a fixed place at a certain time.

When we point to establish context, we do so to get the other person to pay attention with us. There would be no reason, other than mischief, to have a word for what is not context. But we might make a mistake. Suzy might make a word "UNIC" to indicate as context all places and times in the world as we know it in which "UNICORN" is a correct description. Alas, Suzy, there aren't any such times and places. If she doesn't agree, then either we can't reason together with this word or else we go along with her to lead her to a contradiction that might convince her that "UNIC" is not a word we can use for context.

These *context words* are quite different from categorematic words. They are not meant to elicit a concept, nor do we use them to describe relative to a context. We assume that each context word does direct us to establishing context, perhaps in a hypothetical scenario. We can add further context words as we talk and reason together in the flow of all, just as we can add further categorematic words.

Using context words to make assertions
When I say "DOG", that's not meant as correct or incorrect unless I supplement it with an indication of some context in which it is meant to be evaluated. I can indicate to you that I mean for it to be evaluated in CRL by writing:

   DOG [CRL]

This is correct iff "DOG" correctly describes in CRL, which is iff in some of CRL there is dog-ing.
   We can form:

   KIWI [NZ]

This is correct iff "KIWI" correctly describes in context NZ, which is iff in some of NZ there is kiwi-ing.
   Let's call these *categorematic words marked for context*. Each is correct or incorrect—no further context is needed. We take each to be an assertion unless we agree that we're considering them only hypothetically.

Ordinary categorematic words used to establish context?
Why not use our ordinary categorematic words to establish context? Why not have:

   TAIL [DONKEY]

This would be correct iff "TAIL" is a correct description in the context established by "DONKEY". But what is that context? The word "DONKEY" is meant to evoke a concept but not one tied to a context, for it can be correct in a context of today in Dogshine and not today in the corral or yesterday in Dogshine. Nor can we use "DOG + CORRAL" or "DOG in CORRAL" in place of "DOG [CRL]", for both of those require a context to be evaluated.

Talking of some of a context
Suppose you assert "RAT [CRL]". But I don't see any rat-ing. So I ask you to point to some of CRL in which "RAT" is a correct description. Suppose you say "RAT [SHD]". I still don't see any rat-ing. So you point to behind the bale of hay. For that context within SHD you make a new context word "BH" and assert "RAT [BH]". O.K., now I see. "RAT" is a correct description in CRL iff it describes correctly in some though not necessarily all of CRL, and we've made that "some" explicit.
   We can't assume that we have a context word for every context within CRL any more than we can assume we have a context word for every context in context of the water in my bath tub. To do so would be to think of "all contexts" within CRL as existing in some way outside our talk and reasoning, whereas "context" is meant for ways we can and do get others to pay attention jointly with us. In a discussion, in reasoning, to direct attention to some of a context that we're considering we make a new context word as needed, especially when we disagree or are puzzled.

Complex categorematic words marked for context
We can form a word,

(DOG + RUN) [PTO]

This is correct iff "DOG + RUN" describes correctly in PTO, and that is iff there's dog-ing in some of the patio this morning. For any categorematic word E we can mark it to be evaluated in a context W by writing: E[W].

Can we combine a word marked for context with a categorematic word? Consider:

(DOG + RUN [PTO]) [CRL]

This would be to link a categorematic word with an assertion. But we use /, +, −, non- , and categorematic linkings to make categorematic words from categorematic words in terms of the concepts those are meant to elicit, not to join a categorematic word with an assertion or to join assertions as in:

(TOY [CRL] / DOG [PTO]) [NZ]

We mark for context an entire categorematic word, base or complex, not its parts.

Compound words marked for context
Suppose we were to have a word:

(1)   (DOG ∧ RUN) [PTO]

This would be correct iff there is dog-ing in the context PTO and running in the context PTO. But that's iff both "DOG [PTO]" and "RUN [PTO]" are correct. So instead of (1) we can use:

DOG [PTO] ∧ RUN [PTO]

This is acceptable since we evaluate a conjunction by whether its parts are correct without invoking concepts. So to mark a conjunction for context we can mark the conjuncts. Then we can mark the conjuncts with different context words, as in:

DOG [PTO] ∧ RUN [CRL]

This is correct iff there is dog-ing in the patio this morning and run-ing in the corral last night: perhaps Birta is in the patio this morning and the sheep were running in the corral last night.

What about negations? Consider:

(¬ CAT) [PTO]

This would be correct iff there is complete absence of cat-ing in the patio this morning. But that's the same condition for this to be correct:

¬ (CAT [PTO])

To mark a negation for context we mark the word that is negated.

Words marked for context If E, F are ordinary categorematic words and W, U are context words, then each of the following is a *word marked for context* or simply a *marked word*:

- E [W]
- E [W] ∧ F [U]
- ¬ (E [W])

Compounds of these using ∧ and ¬ are also marked words.

Any marked word is a correct or an incorrect description. We treat it as an assertion unless we indicate that we are considering it only hypothetically.

We can use marked words to show how our principles of reasoning depend on context. For any categorematic word E we have the principle:

E – (non-E)

This is correct iff every instance of it is correct in any context. Now we can modify the principle to explicitly take account of context:

(E – (non-E)) [W]

We also have the principle:

(2) (E/F) ⊃ E

We understood this as meaning that every instance of it is correct in every context. That is, if an instance of (E/F) is a correct description in a context, so is E. We can make that explicit as a scheme:

(E/F) [W] ⊃ E [W]

An instance of this would be:

(TOY/DOG) [DGS] ⊃ TOY [DGS]

We don't take account of context in (2) with the scheme:

(E/F) [W] ⊃ E [U]

Not all instances of this are correct, for example:

(TOY/DOG) [DGS] ⊃ (TOY) [CRL]

For compound words we have the principle:

B ⊃ (A ⊃ B)

To take account of context we can understand A and B as standing for any marked words. So an instance of this would be:

CAR[SCR] ⊃ (HOUSE [DGS] ⊃ CAR [SCR])

There are other ways we could expand our language of talk in the flow of all to more fully take account of context, as I discuss in Appendix F. But this is enough for our investigations here.

22 Examples

We are not formalizing reasoning from an ordinary language here. We are devising a way to talk about the world from a different perspective than our ordinary language allows. But what we mean by "the world" is not clear. What we think of as the world is surely shaped by the language we use, as I hope to have led you to see. We are not denying that there is something "out there" but insisting that how we see is not a trivial addition to our sensory inputs or a clear lens to see precisely what can be seen in only one way. Still, I have no choice but to give examples in English, either as claims or as descriptions of an experience we might have that we can try to cast in talk of the world as the flow of all.

Example 1 It's raining.

Analysis To interpret this as an assertion we need to specify a context. Let's take that to be SCR, Socorro county, New Mexico. Then we can interpret the example:

> (RAIN) [SCR]

In some of SCR there is raining.

To take account of the time of which the example is meant we might take as context SCRM, Socorro County this morning: (RAIN) [SCRM] .

Example 2 It's not raining.

Analysis If meant as contradicting the last example, we can interpret this as:

> ¬ ((RAIN) [SCRM])

Example 3 It was raining.

Analysis Suppose this is meant to augment Example 1.

We don't have a way to say "some time in the past". If we want to interpret this example we need to describe a context of some time before now, say July 6, 2024, in Luis Lopez, New Mexico, which is within SCR. Let's use "GNID" for that. Then we can interpret the example as:

> RAIN [GNID]

We have no way to say that one context is before another in time.

Example 4 Um ser superior cuida de nos.

Analysis I heard a Brazilian friend say this, which roughly translates as "A superior being takes care of us". The word "ser" is a verb meaning "to be" in the sense of always or a considerable length of time. Here "ser" is made to do duty as a noun. We cannot use "ser" as a base categorematic word because being, existing is how we describe individual things. Consider:

DOG [CRL]

To say this is correct is to say that there is dog-ing going on in CRL, and there is nothing more to say about existing. Similarly for mud-ing and run-ing. There are no assertions of existence but only assertions of categorematic words in context.

To understand a superior being, God, as an individual thing is not compatible with our view of the world as the flow of all. But then much of Western theology is meant to explain how God is not a thing. Here we could adopt "GOD" as a categorematic word that is not tied to time or location any more than "ZOE" is.

Example 5 Birta is barking.

Analysis I said this in the patio one morning. My friend and I could hear my dog Birta barking, probably near the corral. As English speakers we say the example is about Birta, wherever she may be. But in our talk of the flow of all, we have to specify a context to interpret this and Birta does not supply that. We can use:

(BIRTA + BARK) [DGS]

That's because the context of the patio this morning, and the corral, and much more where Birta could be barking are within DGS.

Example 6 Birta is a dog.

Analysis Speaking English we don't take this as meaning Birta is a dog now. We understand it as meaning that Birta has some property, some quality, is a dog in some essential way: Birta-ing is dog-ing. In that case we should interpret the example as a scheme:

(BIRTA) [W] $\supset$ (BIRTA + DOG) [W]

In any context in which "BIRTA" is correct, so is "BIRTA + DOG". That can only be if Birta-ing is inseparably mixed with dog-ing. But "any context" is too vague, too unclear for us to use in deciding if a word is a correct description, and equally unclear is "any context word". So, as before, we'll use scenarios to make these phrases clear enough to use.

Scenarios A *scenario* is:

- a general context we agree on for which we have a context word;

- ways we agree can lead us to pay attention together to contexts within the general context so that for each that we consider we have or make a context word;

- evaluations as needed of marked categorematic words as correct or incorrect.

Example 7 Birta is brown. Therefore, something is brown.

Analysis "Birta is brown" is not meant as an assertion of some essential property of Birta. Rather, Birta is brown now; later when she gets old she could be mostly grey. So we don't want to interpret this as a scheme for all contexts.

We can't say that there is something that is brown, only that there is brown-ing. So choosing a context relative to which the example is meant to be evaluated, say PTO, we can interpret this as:

(*) (BIRTA + BROWN) [PTO] ⊃ (BROWN) [PTO]

If we have in mind some context relative to which we intend to evaluate a word, and a context word for that, we do not need to further specify a scenario. We need to invoke a scenario only to clarify what we mean by "every context". For example, we can say that (*) is correct as an instance of a principle for evaluating together-uses:

(E + F) [W] ⊃ F [W]

We understand this as meaning that every instance of it is correct in any scenario.

Example 8 Every rat is brown.

Analysis In a scenario we could assert a scheme

(RAT) [W] ⊃ (RAT + BROWN) [W]

But this would be correct if in each context we're considering there are lots of rats, some white and some brown. We need to say that there is no rat-ing that is not brown.

(RAT) [W] ⊃ ((RAT + BROWN) [W] ∧ ¬ (RAT + non-BROWN) [W])

But this could be correct if there is no rat-ing in the scenario. To add that there is some rat-ing in the scenario, suppose we have a context word "GSN" to stand for the general context of the scenario. Then we can form the scheme of assertions:

(RAT) [GSN] ∧

(RAT) [W] ⊃ ((RAT + BROWN) [W] ∧ ¬ (RAT + non-BROWN) [W])

Example 9 Some rats are brown and some rats are not brown.

Analysis This is correct iff there is rat-ing in the scenario, and not all rat-ing is brown and not all rat-ing is non-brown:

(RAT + BROWN) [GSN] ∧ (RAT + (non-BROWN)) [GSN]

Example 10 Unicorns don't exist.

Analysis In our thing-talk we become confused trying to reason with this, asking what it is that doesn't exist. Here we can interpret the example in a scenario with a scheme with W standing for any context word we use in the scenario:

¬ ((UNICORN) [W])

96   *Chapter 22*

If we understand the example to be for the world as it is, was, and will be, rather than a hypothetical context, we could use "WRLD" to stand for that as context and interpret the example as:

    ¬ ((UNICORN) [WRLD])

But then we should give a way for specifying contexts in the world as we know it along with context words. Not likely.

Example 11   Dick to Tom: Be careful. *The paint there is wet.*

Analysis   Suppose Dick and Tom are in Dick and Zoe's yard today, for which we can make a context word "DZY". Then we can interpret the example as:

(a)   (PAINT + WET) [DZY]

This is to take "WET" as a categorematic word: look, see, WET. There can be wet-ing, though in English we demand that "wet" describe some stuff: wet paint, wet cat, wet weather. I think (a) is preferable to "(PAINT / WET) (DZY)" because "WET" is a correct description in DZY, which we have as a consequence of (a).

Example 12   Tom to Dick: The paint there is drying.

Analysis   Taking this as supplementing the last example, we can interpret it:

    (PAINT + DRY) [DZY]

This is good if we understand "DRY" as a process, dry-ing, which is a reading compatible with our view of the world as the flow of all. But then how can we interpret what Dick said later to Tom: "The paint is dry"?

In English we distinguish between drying and being dry. We might construe "dry" as an adjective to mean the completion of the process of drying. But there are many contexts in which we talk of dry without assuming that the dryness is the end result of some drying: I pet Arfito now and say that he's dry without thereby invoking the end of becoming dry. It seems we need a categorematic word for being dry and not the process of drying and not the end of a process of drying.

We don't have this problem with "DOG", for we don't have in English an idea of becoming dog as opposed to being dog. Perhaps, though, we have this problem with "RED", for we have in English the word "reddening" for becoming red as opposed to being red.

Example 13   Leucippus . . . proclaimed that empty space—or the void—exists and that the atoms move in it. This was a revolutionary assertion for his day, since it was tantamount, in the language of the times, to maintaining the existence of that in which nothing exists.
                    B.A.G. Fuller and Sterling M. McMurrin, *A History of Philosophy*, p. 88

Analysis   The oddity here is using the word "exists" for describing the void, as if it were a thing. In the flow of all we don't talk of a void as a thing, nor do we talk of things or masses existing. We can't even say that there is a context in which no base categorematic word is correct.

Example 14 Snow is white.

Analysis For a scenario we can interpret this with a scheme where W stands for any context word we use in the scenario:

SNOW [W] ⊃ (SNOW + WHITE) [W]

In some scenarios this is correct. In some it is not correct, for example with a word W meant to indicate as context a curb of a busy street in New York three days after a snow fall.

If the example is meant, however, as an assertion about the inherent nature of snow, it is an abstraction in the same way a scientific law is an abstraction. It serves as a guide to us in our understanding of the world: if we ignore all of the stuff we pick up on the sidewalk in New York three days after it snowed except for the crystalline part, if we ignore the soot and dust that is mixed with it, then that stuff is white. The crystalline part is what we take to be "really" snow, in the first step of scientific analysis.[10] I don't see how to make such assertions based on abstractions in our talk of the flow of all. But then I don't see how to formulate scientific abstractions in modern formal logic.

Example 15 Swimming is fun.

Analysis Suzy believes this. But swimming isn't always fun, as Dick knows from when he fell out of a canoe and had to swim in cold water and was exhausted when he arrived at the shore. We also say:

Running is good exercise.

Dieting is difficult.

These are not meant as assertions for all contexts, nor as telling us how to use words. Nor are they meant as abstractions. They're rough generalizations: all else being equal, swimming is fun for me, running is good exercise for most people most of the time, dieting is usually difficult for most people. I don't see how to interpret this in our talk of the flow of all.

Example 666 Cat-ing is evil-ing.

Analysis What's meant here is not that each individual cat is evil, for we know from *The BARK of DOG* that any cat can be brought to realize love, to be loving in the world. Rather, it is the nature of cat-ing that is evil. So we don't want to interpret this as a scheme correct in every scenario:

(a)   CAT [W] ⊃ (CAT + EVIL) [W]

Here, where Griselda is holding her loving cat on her lap, there is no evil mixed,

---

[10] See my "Models and Theories" for a fuller discussion of this view of science.

though there is always the potential for evil in her cat, for that is the nature of cat-ing. Nor can we use:

(b)   CAT [W] ⊃ EVIL [W]

This could be correct in a scenario, even in the world as we know it, if it turns out to be just coincidence that evil-ing always accompanies cat-ing, a cosmic coincidence that we with our limited powers have thought of as part of cat-ing.

    This example is about the nature of cat-ing, and at best we can view it as an assertion about the meaning of "CAT". But I see no way beyond (a) and (b) to talk of that in the flow of all.

23 Forms of Words

Vocabulary
- *Base categorematic words*
- *Context words*
- *Local connectives* /, +, −, non-, categorematic linkings
- *Global connectives* ⌐, ∧
- *Parentheses* ( )
- *Square brackets* [ ]

Categorematic words and compound words
These are defined as in Chapter 13. And as before, if A and B are any words:

$A \vee B \equiv_{Def} \neg(\neg A \wedge \neg B)$

$A \supset B \equiv_{Def} \neg(A \wedge \neg B)$

Words marked for context
- For any categorematic word E and context word W, E [W] is a word *marked for context*, or simply a *marked word*.
  We read it as "E in W", or "E relative to W".
- For any marked categorematic word E [W], (¬ E [W]) is a *marked compound word*.
- For any marked categorematic words E [W] and F [U], (E [W] ∧ F [U]) is a marked compound word.
- For any marked word A, (¬ A) is a marked compound word.
- For any marked words A and B, (A ∧ B) is a marked compound word.

Schemes of words
Word schemes Any concatenation of capital letters, lower case letters, local connectives, global connectives, parentheses, square brackets according to the rules for forming words is a *scheme* of words. It is a *compound word scheme* if only ¬, ∧, and possibly square brackets, and capital letters appear in it.

Instantiation of a scheme An *instantiation* of a word scheme is the result of:
- Replacing each lower-case letter in it with a categorematic linking, where every occurrence of that lower-case letter in the scheme is replaced by the same categorematic linking;
- Replacing each capital letter in it that is flanked by square brackets with

a context word, where every occurrence of that capital letter in the scheme is replaced by the same context word;

- Replacing each capital letter in it that is not flanked by square brackets with a word, categorematic if flanked by a local connective, where every occurrence of that letter in the scheme is replaced by the same word.

An instantiation of a scheme an *instance* of the scheme.

Every word is an instantiation of some scheme of words   Any concatenation is a word iff there is some scheme of words of which it is an instance.

Schemes of words marked for context   A *scheme of words marked for context* is a scheme any instantiation of which is a word marked for context.

Schemes of words marked for a single context   A *scheme of words marked for a single context* is a scheme of words marked for context in which only one letter is used throughout to stand for a context word.

Two or more schemes of words marked for context are *marked for a single context* if only one letter is used in all the schemes to stand for a context word.

Open instantiation of a scheme of words marked for context   An *open instantiation* of a scheme of words marked for context is defined just as an instantiation of the scheme except that letters that stand for context words are not replaced by context words.

Compatible instantiations of schemes of words marked for context   Given two or more schemes of words marked for context, instantiations of those are compatible if any lower-case letter that appears in one of the schemes is replaced by the same categorematic linking in all the schemes, any letter in square brackets is replaced by the same context word in all the schemes, and any upper-case letter not in square brackets that appears in one of the schemes is replaced by the same word that is not a context word in all the schemes.

An *open* compatible instantiation of schemes of words marked for context is defined the same except that letters for context words are not replaced by context words.

Example 1 ((E + F) / G)

((¬ (F – G)) ∧ (G / H))

((F $\underline{c}$ E) – (G + H))

Analysis   Each of these is a scheme of words.

Example 2   (A ∧ B) ∧ ¬ C

Analysis   This is a compound word scheme.

Chapter 23

Example 3 E [W]

Analysis This is a scheme of marked words. Here is an instantiation of it:

(HOUSE) [DGS]

Here is another instantiation of it:

(SHEEP – GOAT) [DGS]

Example 4 E [W] ∧ F [U]

Analysis This is a compound scheme of marked words. Here is an instantiation:

(BARK) [PTO] ∧ (SHEEP) [CRL]

Example 5 E [W] ∧ F [W]

Analysis This is a scheme of words marked for a single context. Here is an instantiation of it:

(BARK) [CRL] ∧ (SHEEP) [CRL]

Example 6 (E [W] ∧ F [W]) ⊃ G [U]

(E [W] ∧ F [W]) ⊃ G [W]

Analysis The first is a compound scheme of words marked for context but not for a single context. Here is an instantiation of it:

((DONKEY) [CRL] ∧ (SHEEP) [CRL]) ⊃ (DOG [DGS])

The second is a compound scheme of words that is marked for a single context. Here is an instantiation of it:

((DONKEY) [CRL] ∧ (SHEEP) [CRL]) ⊃ (DOG [CRL])

Note that this latter is also an instantiation of the first scheme. We do not require that different letters for context words be replaced by different context words.

Example 7 (E + F) [W] ∧ (G – (H [W])) [W]

Analysis This is not a scheme of words: a local connective cannot join a categorematic word with a marked categorematic word.

Example 8 (E + F) [W] ∧ (G – H) [W]

(E c F) [U] ∧ ¬ ((G – H) [U])

Analysis Each of these is a scheme of words marked for a single context. But they are not together marked for a single context. Here is a compatible instantiation of them:

(DONKEY + BROWN) [CRL] ∧ (HAY – STRAW) [CRL]

(DONKEY directed towards BROWN) [NZ] ∧ ¬ ((HAY – STRAW) [NZ])

Example 9   (E + F) [W]

Analysis   Here is an open instantiation of this scheme:

    (DONKEY + BROWN) [W]

Example 10   (E + F) [W]

    (G c H) [W] ⊃ (E [W])

Analysis   These two schemes together are marked for a single context. Here are compatible instantiations of them:

    (SHEEP + BROWN) [CRL]

    ((DONKEY <u>directed towards</u> DOG) [CRL]) ⊃ (SHEEP [CRL])

Here is an open compatible instantiation of them:

    (SHEEP + BROWN) [W]

    ((DONKEY <u>directed towards</u> DOG) [W]) ⊃ (SHEEP [W])

24 How Words Can Be Used to Describe

Categorematic words elicit concepts
Categorematic words elicit concepts as set out in Chapter 14.

Context words stand for contexts
Each context word stands for a context.

Correct descriptions
If E and F are categorematic words, ordinary or local, and W is a context word:

- If E is a base ordinary categorematic word, E[W] is a correct description iff E is a correct description in context W.

- (E / F) [W] is a correct description iff E is a correct description in W in a way modified by our understanding of F.

- (E + F + . . . + H) [W] is a correct description iff each of E, F, . . . , H is a correct description in W and they describe in a joined, mixed, together way in which E, F, . . . , H cannot describe as separated spatially (conceptually).

- For any categorematic linking $\underline{c}$, (E $\underline{c}$ F) [W] is a correct description iff each of E and F is a correct description in W and and the two words describe together in a way peculiar to this linking.

- (E – F – . . . – H) [W] is a correct description iff E is a correct description in W, or F is a correct description in W, . . . , or H is a correct description in W.

- (non-E) [W] is a correct description iff E does not describe correctly in some of W.

Marked compound words

- ¬ A is a correct description iff A is not a correct description.

- A ∧ B is a correct description in a context iff A is a correct description and B is a correct description.

25 Inferences and Validity

Recall the definitions of inference, valid inference, and valid word from Chapter 17 for which no context words are in the language.

> An *inference* is two or more words, one of which is designated the *conclusion* and the others the *premises*, that is intended by the person who sets it out as either showing that the conclusion follows from the premises or investigating whether that is the case. The order of the premises does not matter.
>
> An inference is *valid* means that in any context in which each of the premises is a correct descriptions, so is the conclusion. If an inference is not valid, it is *invalid*.
>
> A word is *valid* means that in any context it is a correct description.

Consider, then, the following inference:

(1) (DOG + RUN)
     Therefore (DOG)

This is valid: in any context in which the premise is a correct description, the conclusion is a correct description. Now we can make explicit that this evaluation depends on context by using a scheme, where W stands for a context word:

(2) (DOG + RUN) [W]
     Therefore (DOG) [W]

For example, if "(DOG + RUN) [DGS]" is correct, so is "(DOG) [DGS]". In evaluating inferences for validity we took account of context implicitly before and explicitly now.

We can generalize from (2) to a scheme of inferences:

(3) (E + F) [W]
     Therefore (E) [W]

We can say that this is valid because no matter what categorematic words E and F stand for, and no matter what context word W stands for, if the first is correct, the second is, too.

These examples suggest the following modification of our definitions of inference and validity.

Schemes of inferences marked for context
A *scheme of inferences marked for context* is two or more schemes of words marked for context, one of which is designated the *conclusion* scheme and the others the *premise* schemes, which is intended by the person who sets it out as

either showing that the conclusion follows from the premises or investigating whether that is the case. The order of the premises does not matter.

An *open scheme of inferences* is defined similarly except each premise and the conclusion is an *open instantiation* of a scheme of words marked for context.

A scheme of inferences or an open scheme of inferences is *marked for a single context* if only one letter stands for a context word in the premises and conclusion.

So (3) is a scheme of inferences marked for a single context, and (2) is an open scheme of inferences.

In what follows we will be concerned with only schemes of inferences marked for a single context. In Appendix F, I discuss how we might evaluate schemes of inferences that are marked for more than one context.

To define what we mean by a valid inference scheme we use scenarios.

Valid schemes of inferences A scheme of inferences or an open scheme of inferences is *valid in a scenario* iff for any compatible instantiation of the schemes in it, if the instantiations of the premises are correct in the scenario, then the instantiation of the conclusion is correct in the scenario.

A scheme of inferences is *valid* iff it is valid in every scenario.

We can also talk of a valid scheme of words. Consider:

   (DOG + RUN) [W] ⊃ (DOG) [W]

This is correct in any scenario because of our principle:

   (E + F) [W] ⊃ (E) [W]

Consider also:

   (CAT − (non-CAT)) [W]

This is valid because of our principle:

   (E − (non-E)) [W]

Valid schemes of words A scheme of words or an open scheme of words is *valid in a scenario* iff any instantiation of it is correct in the scenario.

A scheme of words is *valid* iff it is valid in every scenario.

We now use these notations for schemes and open schemes of words.

R, S, T, and other bold-face capital letters stand for scenarios.

A, B, ... ⊨$_S$ C   the inference scheme A, B, ... *therefore* C is valid in scenario **S**

Chapter 25

$A, B, \ldots \vDash C$ the inference scheme $A, B, \ldots$ *therefore* C is valid

$\vDash_S A$ the word scheme or open word scheme A is valid in scenario S

$\vDash A$ the word scheme or open word scheme A is valid

We write $\nvDash$ for "is not valid" and $\nvDash_S$ for "is not valid in scenario S".

We have as before the reduction of valid inferences to valid words.

Validity of inferences reduced to validity of words

$A \vDash B$ iff $\vDash A \supset B$

$A, \ldots, B, C \vDash D$ iff $A, \ldots, B \vDash (C \supset D)$

---

26 A System for Reasoning with Words Marked for Context, WMC

We modify the system **IXN** for deriving valid words and valid inferences from Chapter 20.

E, F, G, H, K, L stand for categorematic words.
W stands for a context word.

Initial schemes of words

a. (E/F) [W] ⊃ E [W]

b. (E/E) [W] ⊃ E [W]

c. E [W] ⊃ (E/E) [W]

d. (E + F + ... + H) [W] ⊃ K [W]
   where K is one of E, F, ..., H

e. (E + F + ... + H) [W] ⊃ L [W]
   where L is a together-use of some but not necessarily all
   of E, F, ..., H, in any order, possibly more than once

f. L [W] ⊃ (E + F + ... + H) [W]
   where L is a together-use in which each of E, F, ..., H appears,
   in any order, possibly more than once

g. (E c̲ F) [W] ⊃ E [W]

h. (E c̲ F) [W] ⊃ F [W]

i. K [W] ⊃ (E − F − ... − H) [W]
   where K is one of E, F, ..., H

j. L ⊃ (E − F − ... − H)
   where L is a disjoining of some but not necessarily all of
   E, F, ..., H, in any order, possibly more than once

k. (E − F − ... − H) [W] ⊃ L [W]
   where L is a disjoining in which each of E, F, ..., H appears,
   in any order, possibly more than once

l. (E − E) [W] ⊃ E [W]

m. (non-(non-E)) [W] ⊃ E [W]

n. E [W] ⊃ (non-(non-E)) [W]

o. $(E - (\text{non-}E))\,[W]$

p. $\neg (E\,[W]) \supset (\text{non-}E)\,[W]$

q. $(E - F)\,[W] \supset (E\,[W] \vee F\,[W])$

r. $(E \vee F)\,[W] \supset (E - F)\,[W]$

s. $\neg (\neg (E\,[W]) \wedge \neg ((\text{non-}E)\,[W]))$

Compound schemes

A, B, C, stand for marked word schemes, where each word marked within them uses the same letter W to stand for a context word.

1. $B \supset (A \supset B)$
2. $(A \supset (B \supset C)) \supset ((A \supset B) \supset (A \supset C))$
3. $(A \wedge B) \supset A$
4. $(A \wedge B) \supset B$
5. $A \supset (B \supset (A \wedge B))$
6. $\neg A \supset (A \supset B)$
7. $(A \supset B) \supset ((\neg A \supset B) \supset B)$

Derivations of words

A derivation of a scheme of words is a sequence of one or more schemes of words ending with that scheme of words in which the order matters and each of the schemes of words in the sequence:

- is an instance of one of the initial schemes (a)–(s) or (1)–(7).
- is an instance of $(E\,[W] \supset F\,[W])$ where $E \approx F$ is derivable in the system for deriving conceptual equivalences **DCE** of Chapter 16.
- follows from one or more of the preceding words by the rule:
    From A and $(A \supset B)$, conclude B.

We call this system for deriving valid words **WMC**, and write:

$\vdash A \equiv_{\text{Def}}$ A is derivable

$\nvdash A \equiv_{\text{Def}}$ A is not derivable

I'll leave to you to show the following.

Derivable words are valid If $\vdash A$, then $\vDash A$.

Derivation of an inference An scheme of inferences or open inferences A, B, C, ... *therefore* D is derivable in **WMC** means that there is a derivation of scheme D in **WMC** supplemented by schemes A, B, C, ... That is, the following clause is added to the definition of "derivation":

- is one of A, B, C, ...

If there is such a derivation, we write:

    A, B, C, ... ⊢ D

We write ⊬ for "is not derivable".

    I'll leave to you to show the following.

Derivable inferences are valid
    If A, B, C, ... ⊢ D, then A, B, C, ... ⊨ D.

Derivability of inferences reduced to derivability of words
    A ⊢ B iff ⊢ (A ⊃ B)
    A, ..., B, C ⊢ D iff A, ..., B ⊢ (C ⊃ D)

Transitivity of derivability If A ⊢ B and B ⊢ C, then A ⊢ C.

27 Local Categorematic Words

I can direct your attention to dog-ing this morning in the patio by asserting:

(1) DOG [PTO]

That's correct. As you look, you form a concept of dog-ing restricted to this morning in the patio. We can make a new categorematic word from (1) meant to elicit that concept:

(2) [[DOG [PTO]]]

This is meant to elicit our concept of "DOG" relative to context PTO. It is a local version of "DOG", a local categorematic word. It does not pick out "the dog-ing" now in the patio. Rather, it conveys to us a concept that allows us to focus our attention in the same way as "DOG [PTO]" does.

We can assert that (2) is a correct description in the context of last night in the corral:

(3) [[DOG [PTO]]] [CRL]

That happens to be correct. But that's not to say there is the same dog-ing in the patio now as there was in the corral last night. That would be to slip into thing-talk, as if there is a dog-ing now and here and a dog-ing then and there. It's just that the local categorematic word (2) correctly describes in the patio now and in the corral last night. It could be that only Birta is in the patio now, while last night she and Bidú were in the corral.

The word (2) elicits a restricted, local concept of dog-ing. That's dog-ing, too. So for any context word W,

[[DOG [PTO]]] [W] ⊃ DOG [W]

In particular from (3) being correct, the following is correct

DOG [CRL]

So we can form:

[[DOG [CRL]]]

And then the following is a correct description of last night in the corral:

[[DOG [CRL]]] [CRL]

But the following would not be correct since both Bidú and Birta were in the corral last night and only Birta is in the patio this morning:

[[DOG [CRL]]] [PTO]

Likewise, if it rained last night and there was a lot of mud in the corral but this morning most of it has dried up, the following would not be correct. So using "CRLM" for context of the corral this morning:

[[MUD [CRL]]] [CRLM]

A local categorematic word is meant to elicit the concept of all dog-ing, mud-ing, run-ing in the context on which it is based.[11]

Let's cast this discussion more generally.

Local categorematic words Given a marked categorematic word E[W], we can form a categorematic word [[E[W]]]. It is meant to elicit the concept of E in the context W.

If U is a context word, and [[E[W]]] [U] is correct, then E[U] is correct:

[[E[W]]] [U] ⊃ E[U]

And if E[W] is correct, then [[E[W]]] is a correct description in W:

E[W] ⊃ [[E[W]]] [W]

Mistakes

You might think that there's some sheep-ing in the corral now and assert:

(4) [[SHEEP [CRLM]]]

But I've moved them to the pasture. So should we say that (4) is not a word?

Think of the sheep-ing in the corral this morning. There is none. Does that concept yield a correct description in CRLM? In DZY? No, it's not correct in any context. That is, "[[SHEEP [CRLM]]]" is null. But we can allow (4) as a word since, just as "PEGASUS", it elicits a concept.

Mistaken local categorematic words A local categorematic word [[E[W]]] is *mistaken* if E[W] is not a correct description. A mistaken local categorematic word is *null*: for any context word U, [[E[W]]] [U] is not correct.

¬ E[W] ⊃ ¬ [[E[W]]] [U]

Why not avoid mistaken categorematic words by requiring that in order for "[[E[W]]]" to be a word E[W] must be correct? If we did we couldn't first set out the forms of words and then consider the conditions for them to be correct descriptions, which would create circularity or worse.[12] But we can avoid using a mistaken

---

[11] Some colleagues were puzzled how an assertion could be made into a description. But we do that in our ordinary speech. For example, suppose you're at my home with me and I say:

There are dogs in the front yard.

Later I tell you:

The dogs that were in the front yard are now in the backyard.

[12] Compare "On the Error in Frege's Proof that Names Denote".

local word as a basis for a local word, such as "[[[[SHEEP [CRLM]]] [PTO]]] ", by requiring that for any ordinary categorematic word E and context words W and U, "[[[[E [W]]] [U]]] " is not a word. Generally, [[E [W]]] is not a word if [[and]] appear in E.

Since "[[SHEEP [CRLM]]] " is null, it follows that "DOG + [[SHEEP [CRLM]]] " is null: if it weren't, then in any context W for which DOG + [[SHEEP [CRLM]]] [W] is correct, "[[SHEEP [CRLM]]] [W]" would be correct, too. In contrast, consider:

IDEA / [[SHEEP [CRLM]]]

This elicits a concept, since "[[SHEEP [CRLM]]] " elicits a concept. And it could be correct. That a local categorematic word is null does not mean that every categorematic word in which it appears is null. Again, consider "PEGASUS".

Change

Suppose the following are correct:

([[DOG [PTO]]] + AWAKE) [PTO]

([[DOG [PTO]]] + SLEEP) [CRL]

This doesn't mean that all dog-ing last night in the corral was mixed with sleep-ing, for Bidú could have been awake and alert for coyotes. Nor does it mean that Birta has one property now and had a different property last night. Rather, we can describe correctly with the local categorematic word "[[DOG [PTO]]] " for both this morning in the patio and last night in the corral, and for now in the patio it's correct to assert that word together with "AWAKE", and for last night in the corral it's correct to assert that word together with "SLEEP". The "sameness" and the "change" are not in what is described but in the descriptions that are applicable.

Suppose I direct your attention to an odd smell now in the patio with:

SMELL [PTO]

Then I can say that "the same smell" was in the corral last night:

[[SMELL [PTO]]] [CRL]

And suppose that the following is correct:

([[SMELL [PTO]]] + WIND) [PTO])

∧ ([[SMELL [PTO]]] + WATER) [CRL]

That does not mean that a thing that's now in the patio had one property and in the corral last night it had another, unless you think that any time we use "this", as in "this smell", we have to be talking about a thing with properties.

We can combine a local categorematic word with any categorematic word in all the ways we can combine ordinary categorematic words. For example:

[[SMELL [PTO]]] / SKUNK

non-[[SMELL [PTO]]]

[[SMELL [PTO]]] + [[DOG [PTO]]]

Descriptive equivalence of local categorematic words
Suppose that both of the following are correct:

[[BIRD (PTO)]] [CRL]

[[BIRD (CRL)]] [PTO]

Since "[[BIRD (PTO)]]" describes bird-ing this morning in the patio and is correct describing last night in the corral, and "[[BIRD (CRL)]]" describes bird-ing last night in the corral and is correct describing now in the patio, these words are equivalent for describing even though they elicit different concepts because of the context words they use. That is,

"[[BIRD [PTO]]]" ≡ "[[BIRD [CRL]]]"

"[[BIRD [PTO]]]" ≠ "[[BIRD [CRL]]]"

The idea that local categorematic words cannot be equivalent if they are given relative to context words that describe disjoint locations is a holdover from thing-talk. We're not talking about the same bird-ing or the same smell, but whether a particular description, relative to some time and place, is apt.

Equivalent local categorematic words If [[E [W]]] [U] and [[E [U]]] [W] are correct assertions, then "[[E [W]]]" ≡ "[[E [U]]]". That is, for any context word V,

[[E [W]]] [V] is a correct description iff [[E [U]]] [V] is a correct description.

([[E [U]]] [W] ∧ [[E [W]]] [U]) ⊃

([[E [U]]] [V] ⊃ [[E [W]]] [V])

The same?
What do we mean by "the same"? What do we mean by saying that the same smell-ing that's in the patio now was in the corral last night? The same run-ing? What is the same dog-ing?

What we mean by "the same" is fundamental, whether talking of things or in the flow of all. In thing-talk we become tongue-tied trying to say what we mean by identity, by this thing here being the same as that thing we talked about earlier. We talk about properties of "the thing", and essential properties, but really all we can do is try to draw out some important characteristics of the notion, not reduce it to any other notion. Here, focusing on whether a concept established relative to a context is applicable in another context we can try to circumscribe with various assumptions what we mean by "the same". But our intuitions that guide us will be influenced by our experiences as thing-language speakers. We are tourists, hoping that some day someone from a mass-process language culture will show up to guide us.

Whatever this notion of sameness is, it is not an identity of things, even if what we are talking about in our process language would be characterized as a thing by speakers of English. There is no idea here of unchanging stability, for all is flow. What we have are words we use for descriptions, and sometimes a local version of one can be understood to apply in another context.

28 Examples: Stability and Change

Example 1 (Suzy in Dick and Zoe's yard) This dog existed here three years ago.

Analysis Recall that we have the context word "DZY" for Dick and Zoe's yard now. Let's use "DZYA" as a context word to stand for Dick and Zoe's yard three years ago. Then we can interpret what Suzy said as an assertion:

   [[DOG [DZY]]] [DZYA]

That's all there is to talk of existence in this example.

   This is not an assertion that the dog-ing in Dick and Zoe's yard now is the same as the dog-ing three years ago in Dick and Zoe's yard. Maybe Wanda brought her chihuahua over that day to play with Spot. But Spot-ing is in the yard now and was in the yard three years ago. In that case, the following would not be a correct description:

(a) [[DOG [DZYA]]] [DZY]

But if Spot-ing had been the only dog-ing in their yard three years ago, (a) would be correct, and in that case we'd have " [[DOG [DZY]]] " $\equiv$ "[[DOG [DZYA]]] ". But this could be correct whether as a description of one dog or many dogs, dead or alive, or served on a platter.

Example 2 Dick asks Zoe why she's screwing up her nose. She says she smells the same skunk odor that was here yesterday.

Analysis Suppose we have words:

   FN for context where Zoe is speaking in the forest now

   FY for context yesterday where Zoe is speaking now in the forest

Then we can interpret what Zoe said:

   (ZOE + SMELL) <u>directed towards</u> (ODOR/SKUNK)) [FN]

   $\wedge$ [[(ODOR/SKUNK) [FN]]] [FY]

   We have no way to talk of before and after in our assertions except through our choice of context words.

Example 3 If we take some ice cubes from the refrigerator, crush them, and put them into a glass of coke, we may say:

   The ice in the coke is the same ice that was in the refrigerator before.[13]

Analysis Let "RFRG" be a context word for in the refrigerator a few minutes ago and let "GLS" be a context word to stand for in the glass now. Then we can interpret the example as:

---

[13] From Harry C. Bunt, *Mass Terms and Model Theoretic Semantics*, p. 36.

116   Chapter 28

$$[[\text{ICE [RFRG]}]] [\text{GLS}] \wedge [[\text{ICE [GLS]}]] [\text{RFRG}]$$

$$\wedge\ (\text{ICE}) [\text{RFRG}] \supset (\text{ICE} + \text{CUBE}) [\text{RFRG}]$$

$$\wedge\ (\text{ICE}) [\text{GLS}] \supset (\text{ICE} + \text{CRUSH}) [\text{GLS}]$$

Only through the description of contexts can we note before and after, here and there.

Example 4 The water in the pond in my patio is part of all water.

Analysis Some people who analyze talk of masses in ordinary English say that "water" is a mass-term that refers to all water at all times and places, so that the example is correct.[14] But this seems too broad, a confusion of the term "water" being a correct description at various times and places with the wish to have something corresponding to it, almost an abstract entity, which is at all those times and places. We do not say that my dog Birta is part of all dogs that are at all times and places. We might, if we are platonists, say there is a thing that is the collection of all dogs at all times and places and Birta is part of that, but to do so is a long way from our ordinary talk and demands a great deal of metaphysics beyond what most of us find plausible or necessary to explain the truth of what we say. In the view of the world as the flow of all, "WATER" is a categorematic word we use for descriptions in contexts. To say that this water here and now is part of all water is to say no more than that "WATER" is a correct description of here and now.[15]

Example 5 What Kim spilled is the same coffee as Sandy wiped up.[16]

Analysis Let's use word "KS" to stand for a context of when and where Kim spilled coffee, and "SW" to stand for a context of when and where Sandy wiped up coffee. Then we can interpret the example:

$$(((\text{KIM} + \text{SPILL})\ \underline{\text{directed towards}}\ \text{COFFEE}) [\text{KS}]$$

$$\wedge\ ((\text{SANDY} + \text{WIPE})\ \underline{\text{directed towards}}\ \text{COFFEE}) [\text{SW}]$$

$$\wedge\ [[\text{COFFEE (KS)}]] [\text{SW}] \wedge [[\text{COFFEE (SW)}]] [\text{KS}]$$

Example 6 Dick: This mud used to be brown.

Analysis Not only things change. Suppose we have a context word "DS" for where Dick is now speaking, and Dick provides us with a word "UB" for context where the mud was previously. These need not overlap in space, since the mud could have been in a place in a yard and scooped up and carried to make an adobe brick in another place in that yard. Then we can interpret the example as:

---

[14] Willard van Orman Quine says in *Word and Object:*
> There is no reason to boggle at water as a single though scattered object, the aqueous part of the world. p. 98

[15] Harry C. Bunt in *Mass Terms and Model-Theoretic Semantics* presents a theory of parts for masses which is based on an atemporal, alocational conception of mass.

[16] The example comes from "Mass Expressions" by F. J. Pelletier and L. K. Schubert, p. 359.

([[MUD [DS]]] + BROWN) [UB]

∧ ¬ (([[MUD [UB]]] + BROWN) [DS])

∧ [[MUD [DS]]] [UB] ∧ [[MUD [UB]]] [DS]

Again, the only way we take account of before and after ("used to be") is by how we specify contexts.

Example 7 This running used to be fast.

Analysis What we conceive of as process in our ordinary talk can change, too. Dick could have started running fast and slowed down after 20 meters. I'll let you interpret this.

Example 8 All is change.

Analysis We can formulate talk of what we can describe with a local word with changing descriptions. But change as endemic, change as the nature of the flow of all, is incoherent, for there is no *that* to change. There is only talk of the flow of all under specific descriptions and further descriptions which in contexts can apply or not apply.

Example 9 Dick and Zoe are walking in the forest. Dick says to Zoe:

   The river is very deep here. Don't step into it.

Analysis Dick talks of the river as a thing when he says "the river". But rivers are changing, flowing. Zoe, getting the hang of thinking of the world as the flow of all, quotes Heraclitus:

   You can't step into the same river twice.

Then Tom who is along with them butts in:

   River? What river?

He's right that in viewing the world as the flow of all a river is not a thing. But we can talk of the river by making a word "DZTW" for a context where they are talking:

   [[RIVER [DZTW]]]

We can even talk of stepping into the river:

   ((ZOE + STEP) into [[RIVER [DZTW]]]) [DZTW]

But to say that Zoe steps into the river twice would require a way to count, and it is things we count. We would also need a way to say "any time in the future" in order to deny that it is possible to step in the river twice. Heraclitus's dictum is directed towards those who speak a thing-language.

Example 10 Dick had the same idea as Suzy.

Analysis Ideas need not be things for us to assert sameness. With appropriate context words W and U, we can interpret the example:

(SUZY + IDEA) [W] ∧ (DICK + IDEA) [U]

∧ [[IDEA [W]]] [U] ∧ [[IDEA [U]]] [W]

Example 11 Dick's mind is not the same as Dick's body.

Analysis Talking in the flow of all we can't say that a mind and a body are distinct entities. There is the flow of all, some of which can be described as body-ing and some of which can be described as mind-ing, and a description in the flow might require both those descriptions, but not conceived as two things.

We can say that "MIND" is not conceptually equivalent to "BODY". But that could be so even if "MIND" and "BODY" are descriptively equivalent.

Example 12 There are two patches of mud now in the patio.

Analysis Suppose we have a context word "YIK" to use to describe a context in which what we would say is, in thing-talk, one patch of mud, and "ZIK" for context for the other patch of mud. Then we can say:

(‡) ¬ [[MUD (YIK)]] [ZIK] ∧ ¬ [[MUD (ZIK)]] [YIK]

Descriptions of mud-ing in one context and in the other are not equivalent. So we as English speakers would say that there are two patches of mud.

The word "patches" is a classifier in English with which we can talk of quantities of mud as things we can count. But (‡) would be correct if there were seven patches of mud in YIK and five patches of mud in ZIK.

Example 13 (Dick, shivering in his yard, says to Tom)

This is the same cold we had before.

Analysis We talk in English about the same water, the same dog. But equally we talk about the same cold or the same yellow. I'll let you interpret this.

29 Names Replaced by Descriptions?

In Chapter 3 we agreed that we could use a name from our thing-talk as a categorematic word. To assert "ZOE" about here and now is to say here and now Zoe-ing. Using "DZY" as a context word for Dick and Zoe's yard today, we can assert:

ZOE [DZY]

SPOT [DZY]

There, now, the flux viewed locally as Zoe-ing; there, now, the flux viewed locally as Spot-ing.

Can we use a description of Zoe and abbreviate that as a name rather than using "ZOE" as a categorematic word? In Dick and Zoe's yard now there is woman-ing, so "WOMAN [DZY]" is a correct description. From our thing-talk perspective that's because Zoe is there and no other woman is there. Matilda and her boyfriend Johnny are just outside the gate. Before they go in, Matilda says to Johnny, "See that woman there, that's Zoe." "Oh, I see," says Johnny, "now I know who Zoe is." So it seems that whenever he or Matilda use the name "ZOE", Johnny can understand it as:

(1)   [[WOMAN [DZY]]]

But that's not how Shondel, a friend of Zoe's mother, understands "ZOE". She learned that name when she and Zoe's mother met standing outside a park 15 years ago when Zoe was 8 years old. Let's use "PRK" as a context word for that park when the only female child in the park was Zoe. Then Shondel associates "ZOE" with:

(2)   [[GIRL [PRK]]]

But (1) and (2) can't be equivalent, because in PRK there is no woman-ing, and in DZY there is no girl-ing.

Things, as we conceive of them in English, can have different properties at different times. But conceiving of the world as the flow of all there is no thing that can have those different properties. There are only the descriptions, nothing to "hang them on". We cannot replace names with descriptions.

Can a name used as a categorematic word be correctly applied at two disjoint locations at the same time? Our example of "ZOE" suggests not. But that intuition is based on thinking of "ZOE" picking out a thing, a person, a woman. Even to say that it's picking out woman-ing is to fall into thing-talk. But consider:

SMELL / (PINE + SKUNK + CHOCOLATE)

Let's abbreviate this as "YUCK". It could be a correct description now in both the patio and the corral, which are disjoint locations. Note that I say we abbreviate the word: we give a short way to describe in our experience.

30 A System of Reasoning with Local Words, WMC+Local

We modify the system **WMC** for reasoning with words marked for context to allow for local words.

Let E stand for a categorematic word.
Let W, U, V stand for context words.

Vocabulary
We add to the vocabulary:

- *Double brackets* [[ ]]

Local categorematic words
We define:

> If E is a categorematic word and W is a context word, then [[E [W]]] is a *local categorematic word* or simply a *local word*. It can be used to form complex categorematic words and compound words in any way a categorematic word can except that it cannot appear in a word [[F]].

Categorematic words elicit concepts
Categorematic words elicit concepts as defined in Chapter 14 with the addition:

- [[E [W]]] is meant to elicit the concept of E in the context W.

Principles
We add to the list of initial principles:

i. E [W] ⊃ [[E [W]]] [W]

ii. [[E [W]]] [U] ⊃ E [U]

iii. ¬ (E [W]) ⊃ ¬ ([[E [W]]] [U])

iv. ([[E [U]]] [W] ∧ [[E [W]]] [U]) ⊃
    ([[E [U]]] [V] ⊃ [[E [W]]] [V])

We call this system **WMC+Local** .

Concluding

31 Different Ways of Encountering the World

Individual things via talk of context?
Can we derive talk of individual things in our talk of the flow of all using talk of context?

Suppose you point and assert "DOG" for the context depicted in this picture.

So I'm supposed to pay attention to dog-ing there. But how is that an individual thing? I can't get that idea without already conceiving of the world as made up of things. From a thing-language perspective it's the same dog, the same individual thing depicted in this context:

How does that thing have some properties in the second context different from those in the first? Our method of localizing a categorematic word to some context does not yield individual things, for a local version of "DOG" can describe one dog, seventeen dogs, doggieness, or more.

It seems to me that the idea of an individual thing persisting through its changes cannot be given, extracted, or developed from talk and reasoning about the flow of all.[17]

Individuating from masses in English
In English we use certain words and phrases, called *classifiers*, to pay attention to part of a mass as a thing: "a cup of coffee", "a patch of mud". We can count these: "four cups of coffee", "three patches of mud".

A general, all-purpose classifier in English is "a bit of", though that suggests a small portion. We can say "a bit of water", "a bit of chocolate", "a bit of gold". But

---

[17] Peter Strawson said that in his way of talking without focus on things we could derive talk of individual things if we allow talk of times and locations. In Appendix D I show he's wrong.

it sounds wrong to use "a bit of" with a mass word that isn't meant to describe (from our English-speaking perspective) a substance: "a bit of justice", "a bit of honor". For those we use a different general classifier: "an instance of justice", "an instance of honor". Can we add a general classifier to our talk of the world as the flow of all to have a way to speak of individuals?

Dorothy Lee in "Categories of the Generic and Particular in Wintu" says that in the mass-process language Wintu "particularization" is done by adding a suffix to a "generic" word.

> Particularizations may be used to create a new word, denoting a delimited form of something commonly regarded as generic. p. 144

Lee says that the classifier indicates specific portions of the mass, but is neither singular nor plural. The word *nop* means "deer" in the general mass-process sense, and *nopum* means what we would translate as "one or several deer". This is like what we do with localizing categorematic words in our talk of the flow of all. We particularize but not individualize.

Suppose we were to add to our talk of the flow of all a classifier "a bit of" so that for every categorematic word E, "a bit of E" would be a categorematic word. What individual things would it describe? What bits of snow should "a bit of SNOW" pick out in a scenario for reasoning about shoveling snow from a driveway? Can we identify and re-identify a fall of snow? Is a collection of snow flakes 3 cm in diameter in that drift a bit of snow? Is a collection of flakes that is falling just now a bit of snow? To add an individuating classifier to our talk of the flow of all we'd have to specify what bits of snow, what bits of water, what bits of mud we're talking about in the scenario. Since snow, water, and mud do not come naturally in bits, a general way to specify eludes us. And that's just for mass-process words that are for "substance". What counts as a bit of justice? How can I identify and re-identify some thing that makes "a bit of JUSTICE" a correct description?

Talking about Example 3 of Chapter 28 (p.115), Harry C. Bunt in *Mass Terms and Model Theoretic Semantics* says:

> The choice of an appropriate "individuating standard" must depend on the circumstances; for example, "sugar" will have to be counted as "lumps of sugar" in some contexts, as "grains of sugar" in other contexts, and as "shipments of sugar" in still other contexts. This context-dependence alone makes the proposal [to use sets as the denotation of mass terms] rather unattractive; moreover, it runs into fundamental difficulties, illustrated by [that example]. [It] would be a true sentence about some ice, yet there is no individuating standard in terms of which we can express this, since the identity stated by the sentence is not an identity of any of the pieces of ice involved, but an identity of the totalities of ice made up of whatever pieces are involved.
>
> If context-dependent individuating standards do not work satisfactorily, the next move is naturally to look for context-independent individuating standards.

Such standards would then have to be artificial, since we just saw that natural standards, suggested by the language ("dollop", "lump", "batch", etc.) do not work in general. It is tempting to think of Quine's minimal parts hypothesis and treat mass nouns as denoting the sets of their minimal parts. "Water" would denote the set of H_2O molecules, "furniture" the set of chairs, tables, etc., and "sugar" the set of sugar grains. I have not seen any serious proposal for such an approach, though it would seem to encounter fewer formal difficulties than the use of context-dependent individuating standards. Presumably, this is due to the fact that such a proposal would so obviously run counter to our intuitions. Even if one were to agree with the minimal parts hypothesis, it is often impossible to actually determine a reasonable set of minimal parts. To consider H_2O molecules as the referents of "water" seems counter-intuitive; something like "drops" would seem better, but presents the problem that a drop can be split into smaller drops, so it clearly is not really a minimal part, and the same is true of any other part we can name without making use of technical terms from physics or chemistry. Moreover, for abstract nouns like "leisure", "damage", or "time", for which no minimal parts are assumed to exist, this proposal must fail. pp. 36–37 [18]

Objectivity?

I have not been able to find a way to talk clearly of the world as the flow of all in our thing-language English. Nor have I found a way to talk of individual things in our talk of the flow of all. These ways of seeing the world, of encountering the world, are too different. They are so different that we cannot have a notion of objectivity that covers both kinds of talk. A subjective claim, it is said, is one whose evaluation as true or false, correct or incorrect description, depends on what someone or some thing thinks, believes, or feels; an objective claim is a claim that is not subjective.[19] So Dick says to Snurgy, who is a native speaker of a mass-process language, "There are three cats in the street that were there yesterday." From Snurgy's perspective, the claim is subjective, not describing what is there for all to see, independent of the observer, for it depends on how Dick conceives of cat-ing divided into things that persist in time. Snurgy says, "cat-ing", and Dick is bewildered: seeing cat-ing

---

[18] See my "Models and Theories" for a fuller explanation of why it is wrong to consider water as a collection of H_2O molecules. See also my "Is There a Problem with Formal Semantics for Natural Languages?" for problems with individuating masses.

Here is what Chad Hansen says about individualizing in Chinese in "Individualism in Chinese Thought":

> So, according to Hsün Tzu, spatially distinct stuffs either can be regarded as "two" or can be combined. Further, the same thing can change and still be regarded as "one." Referring to individual objects that persist through time is therefore possible in Chinese. But, unlike English, that is neither the only nor the dominant conceptual scheme in the language. In fact, that Hsün Tzu should have felt it necessary to make this kind of point explicit and that he should have formulated it in the way he did indicates that he regards individuation as an optional and peripheral aspect of a language. p. 46

[19] See my paper with Fred Kroon and William S. Robinson, "Subjective Claims".

is to put Snurgy's view into the description.

What is objective depends on the language we speak which colors if not determines how we view, describe, partition, conceive of what we encounter. There is no language-independent way to classify what is objective that thing-talk speakers and people who talk of the flow of all can use. We have not objectivity but intersubjectivity, shared ways that we reckon describe "what is there" according to our language culture.

*   *   *   *   *   *   *   *

How does my dog Birta encounter the world? Does she conceive of the world as made up of things? Is she encountering the world as the flow of all without partitioning? Pointing to a rabbit I shout "Gavagai", she looks, she chases, sometimes she catches. Is she "seeing" an individual thing or rabbit-ing, following smell with a certainty of a thing she is chasing or chasing in the flow of all?

Woof? Arf? Why can she not tell me? Certainly not now, may she rest in peace.

Appendices

Appendix A Color Words as Process Words or Mass Terms

Others have suggested a view of colors as process or mass, or perhaps we should say color words as mass terms or process words. Here is what Willard van Orman Quine says in *Word and Object*.

> In attributive position next to a mass term the adjective must be taken as a mass term: thus "red" in "red wine". The two mass terms unite to form a compound mass term. When we think of the two component mass terms as singular terms naming two scattered portions of the world, the compound becomes a singular term naming that smaller scattered portion of the world which is just the common part of the two. p. 104

Both Norwood Russell Hanson and Friedrich Waismann, apparently without being aware of each other's work or that of Benjamin Lee Whorf and other linguists, suggested that we could talk of colors as process. In *Patterns of Discovery* Hanson says:

> That it is yellow is a passive thing to say about the sun, as if its colour were yellow as its shape is round and its distance great. Yellow inheres in the sun, as in a buttercup. 'The sun yellows', however, describes what the sun does. As its surface burns, so it yellows. Now the grass would green; it would send forth, radiate greenness—like X-ray fluorescence. Crossing a lawn would be wading through a pool of green light. Colleges would no longer be cold, lifeless stone; now they would emit greyness, disperse it into the courts. As a matter of optics this is rather like what does happen; the change of idiom is not utterly fanciful.
>
>   . . . Speaking of colour-words as verbs just is to think of colours as activities and of things as colouring agents.
>
>   What if information about colours were expressed adverbially? We would then say 'The sun glows yellowly', 'The grass glitters greenly', 'The chapel twinkles greyly'. If everyone spoke thus how could one insist on its being a fact that the sun is yellow, that grass is green, or that the chapel is grey? Could such 'facts' be articulated at all? . . .
>
>   What of primary qualities? 'The sun is round' states a fact. So too 'St John's College hall is rectangular', 'sugar lumps are cubes'.
>
>   Try 'the sun rounds', 'St John's hall rectangulates', 'sugar cubes'. Activity is suggested here. Would one who saw the round sun see the sun rounding? The college hall *is* rectangular. Would this fact be apprehended by a man for whom the hall rectangulates—holding itself in a rectangular form against gravity, wind, cold and damp? Perhaps the man for whom the sun rounds would see the sun incessantly arranging itself as a sphere. If he can say only 'The sun rounds', how else can he see it? pp. 33–34

In "Verifiability" Waismann says:

> People are inclined to think that there is a world of facts as opposed to a world of words which describe these facts. I am not too happy about that. Consider an example. We are accustomed to see colours as a "quality" of objects. That is, colour cannot subsist by itself, but must inhere in a thing. This conception springs from the way we express ourselves. When colour is rendered by an adjective, colour is conceived as an attribute of things, i.e., as something that can have no independent existence. That, however, is not the only way of conceiving of colour. There are languages such as Russian, German,

Italian, which render colour by verbs. If we were to imitate this usage in English by allowing some such form as "The sky blues", we should come face to face with the question, Do I mean the same fact when I say "The sky blues" as when I say "The sky is blue"? I don't think so. We say "The sun shines", "Jewels glitter", "The river shimmers", "Windows gleam", "Stars twinkle", etc.; that is, in the case of phenomena of lustre we make use of a verbal mode of expression. Now in rendering colour phenomena by verbs we assimilate them more closely to the phenomena of lustre; and in doing so we alter not only our manner of speaking but our entire way of apprehending colour. We *see* the blue differently now—a hint that language affects our whole mode of apprehension. In the word "blueing" we are clearly aware of an active, verbal element. On that account, "being blue" is not quite equivalent to "blueing", since it lacks what is peculiar to the verbal mode of expression. The sky which "blues" is seen as something that continually brings forth blueness—it radiates blueness, so to speak; blue does not inhere in it as a mere quality, rather it is felt as the vital pulse of the sky; there is a faint suggestion of the operating of some force behind the phenomenon. It's hard to get the feel of it in English; perhaps it may help you to liken this mode of expression to the impressionist way of painting which is at bottom a new way of seeing: the impressionist sees in colour an immediate manifestation of reality, a free agent no longer bound up with things.

There are, then, different linguistic means of rendering colour. When this is done by means of adjectives, colour is conceived as an attribute of things. The learning of such a language involves for everyone who speaks it his being habituated to see colour as a "quality" of objects. This conception becomes thus incorporated into his picture of the world. The verbal mode of expression detaches colour from things: it enables us to see colour as a phenomenon with a life of its own. Adjective and verb thus represent two different worlds of thought.

There is also an adverbial way of rendering colour. Imagine a language with a wealth of expressions for all shades of lustre, but without adjectives for colours; colours, as a rule, are ignored; *when* they are expressed, this is done by adding an adverb to the world that specifies the sort of lustre. Thus the people who use this sort of language would say, "The sea is glittering golden in the sunshine", "The evening clouds glow redly", "There in the depth a shadow greenly gleams". In such phrases colour would lose the last trace of independence and be reduced to a mere modification of lustre. Just as we in our language cannot say "That's very", but only some such thing as "That's very brilliant", so in the language considered we could not say "that's bluish", but only, e.g., "That's shining bluishly". There can be little doubt that, owing to this circumstance, the users of such language would find it very hard to see colour as a quality of things. For them it would not be the *things* that are coloured, rather colour would reside in the lustre as it glows and darkens and changes—evidence that they would see the world with different eyes.

"But isn't it still true to say that I have the same experience whenever I look up at the sky?" You would be less happy if you were asked, "Do you have the same experience when you look at a picture puzzle and see a figure in it as before, when you didn't see it?" You may perhaps say you see the same lines, though each time in a different arrangement. Now what exactly corresponds to this different arrangement in the case when I look up at the sky? One might say: we are aware of the blue, but this awareness is itself tinged and coloured by the whole linguistic background which brings into prominence or weakens and hides certain analogies. In this sense language does

130   Appendix A

affect the whole manner in which we become aware of a fact: the fact articulates itself differently, so to speak. In urging that you *must* have the same experience whenever you look at the sky you forget that the term "experience" is itself ambiguous: whether it is taken to, e.g., include or to exclude all the various analogies which a certain mode of expression calls up.   pp. 54–56

As suggestive as Waismann's examples are, he is wrong about the use of "blue" as a verb in German and Russian. Neither in German nor Russian is there any sentence we could understand as "The sky blues" in a continual sense of being blue. Russian does allow color words to be turned into verbs as incipients, as we do in English with "to redden" or "to green". We can say "Her face is reddening" for "Her face is turning (becoming) red"; we can say "The field will green" for "The field will turn green". But those uses are not what Waismann is suggesting. However, speakers of Koyukon do speak of color much as Waismann describes, as Melissa Axelrod explains in *The Semantics of Time: Aspectual Categorization in Koyukon Athabascan*, p. 129.

Appendix B Compound Nouns and Meaning

If we look to linguists to understand "doghouse", they'll tell us that it means something like "house for a dog". If we ask them how to understand "cartoon cat" they'll tell us it means something like "cartoon of a cat". There are two problems with this.

First, we want to understand the role that "dog" plays in "doghouse" and the role "cat" plays in "cartoon cat". We don't want a paraphrase or equivalent phrase. Perhaps we can say that "dog" acts like an adjective, and "cat" acts like an adjective. But that's wrong. The word "dog" doesn't act like an adjective; it is an adjective in "doghouse", just as "cat" is in "cartoon cat". We don't have a good explanation of how adjectives mean, how they combine with nouns, nor how adverbs mean, how they combine with verbs. But whatever explanation we do have is exactly what we have for "dog" in "doghouse" and "cat" in "cartoon cat". Linguists give us a list of possibilities for how to understand the link between the two nouns: it could be "for", or "of", or others, as you can see in the quotation below. That list explains and clarifies nothing, for we need to know in advance which of the categories applies for the noun-noun combination, and we can determine that only if we understand the combination. The list does not explain our understanding but only gives us choices for describing our understanding.

The second problem is that giving a paraphrase, or a word or phrase that we can substitute for the phrase, or a definition, does not give the meaning of a word. I've talked about this in "Language-Thought-Meaning". Now I am reminded of a time in 1976 when I was at the logic seminar at Victoria University of Wellington. A senior philosopher was talking about meaning. He was going to explain the meaning of the word "rabbit". So he wrote on the board:

(a)   "Rabbit" means rabbit.

I couldn't understand. I thought he was going to pull a rabbit from his hat to show us, point to it, and say "rabbit". I told him that (a) couldn't be right. But, he said, it's just like with:

(b)   "Rabbit" means lapin.

(The word "lapin" is the usual translation of the word "rabbit" into French.) I still objected. He and the others told me I just didn't understand the subject. I was new to philosophy.

But now that I've thought about it more, I'm sure I was right. Both (a) and (b) involve use-mention confusions. Instead of (b), he should have written:

(c)   "Rabbit" means the same as "lapin".

And likewise (a) should be:

"Rabbit" means the same as "rabbit".

This last gets us nowhere. At least (c) can be used to help us translate.

But we can't carry around rabbits, and dogs, and unicorns to illustrate what we mean. So we give paraphrases, definitions, equivalent phrases to help someone understand what we're saying. Those are aids to help us learn how to use a word or phrase—if we understand the paraphrase or definition. But that route is of no use in explaining the role of a noun used as an adjective: pick which one of these linking phrases that seems most appropriate for this compound. What we need to say about the role of a noun used as an adjective is that it means there is a link, the noun used as a modifier is meant to link the concept of that noun to the referential use of the noun being modified. We can make a list of possibilities for that link, but that will always be incomplete, as linguists have found in expanding the list. However, the idea of a link need not be revised. It is the same with an adjective modifying a noun: it is the concept of the adjective linked to the referential use of the noun.

This is much clearer in talking and reasoning about the world as the flow of all, for we embrace rather than notice as a curious aspect of language that all concept words can play the same roles. There are no verbs, no nouns, no adjectives, no adverbs, but only concept words. Rather than make a list like "dog" (noun), "to dog" (verb), "doggy" (adjective), "doggedly" (adverb), we have the one word "DOG". And then we can have "HOUSE/DOG" for a word that is true in a context if and only if the word "HOUSE" describes correctly and the word "DOG" links that word to the concept of "DOG" in our understanding to apply in that context, where the exact idea of the link depends on our understanding of those two words and, perhaps, the context, an understanding we improve as we use the word more.

* * * * * * * * * * *

Here is an extract from a paper which shows that the description I give of how linguists analyse noun compounds is not a straw man. It is from "On the Semantics of Noun Compounds" by Roxana Girju, Dan Moldovan, Marta Tatu, and Daniel Antohe.

> The semantic interpretation of noun compounds (NCs) deal with the detection and semantic classification of the relations between noun constituents. The problem is complex and has been studied intensively in linguistics, psycho-linguistics, philosophy, and computational linguistics for a long time. There are several reasons that make this task difficult. (a) NCs have implicit semantic relations: for example, "*spoon handle*" encodes a PART-WHOLE relation. (b) NCs' interpretation is knowledge intensive and can be idiosyncratic. For example, to correctly interpret "*GM car*" one has to know that GM is a car-producing company. (c) There can be more than one semantic relation encapsulated in a pair of nouns. For example, "*Texas city*" can be tagged as a PART-WHOLE relation as well as a LOCATION relation. (d) The interpretation of NCs can be highly context-dependent. For example, "*apple juice seat*" can be defined as "seat with apple juice on the table on front of it" (cf. Downing, 1977).
>
> Although researchers (Jespersen, 1954; Downing, 1977) argued that noun compounds encode an infinite set of semantic relations, many agree (Levi, 1978; Finin, 1980) there is a limited number of relations that occur with high frequency in noun compounds. However, the number and the level of abstraction of these frequently used semantic categories are not agreed upon. They can vary from a few prepositional paraphrases (Lauer, 1995) to hundreds and even thousands more specific semantic relations (Finin, 1980). The more abstract the categories, the more noun compounds are covered, but also the more room for variation as to which category a compound should be assigned. Lauer (Lauer, 1995), for example, considers eight prepositional paraphrases as semantic classification categories: *of, for, with, in, on, at, about,* and *from*. According to this classification, the noun compound "*bird sanctuary*", for instance, can be classified both as "*sanctuary* **of** *bird*" and "*sanctuary* **for** *bird*". The main problem with these abstract categories is that much of the meaning of

individual compounds is lost, and sometimes there is no way to decide whether a form is derived from one category or another.

On the other hand, lists of very specific semantic relations are difficult to build as they usually contain a very large number of predicates, such as the list of all possible verbs that can link the noun constituents. Finin (1980), for example, uses semantic categories such as "**dissolved in**" to build interpretations of compounds like "*salt water*" and "*sugar water*". Although, there were several proposals of possible large sets of semantic relations, there has been no attempt to map one set to another, and, more importantly, to define the appropriate level of abstraction for the interpretation of compounds in general, or for a specific application in particular.   pp. 479–480

The authors then proceed to an analysis "using two sets of semantic classification categories: a list of 8 prepositional paraphrases previously proposed by Lauer [reference] and a new set of 35 semantic relations introduced by us."

Here are some problems with this approach beyond what I suggested above.

1. By not seeing the use of a noun in a noun compound as an adjective, it gives no guidance for how to compare, for example, "doggy smell" and "dog smell".

2. The authors do not clarify the relation of noun compounds to noun conjunctions, for example, "dog love" and "dog and love". Indeed, the former is ambiguous: does it mean love for dogs or love by a dog? Yet the latter is clear: there (pointing) is dog and love.

3. The authors do not see that "spoon handle" can be read as not giving a part-whole relation but saying what kind of handle: one for a spoon. That fits into the analysis of modifiers given in my *The Internal Structure of Predicates and Names*.

4. The authors do not realize or at least do not say that their work has application only to noun compounds in English. That's because:

   (a) Prepositions are notoriously difficult to translate into other languages, even into other European languages much less into a language such as Mayan Tzeltal, which Stephen C. Levinson in "Relativity in Spatial Conception and Description" says has only one preposition.

   (b) In some mass-process languages, such as Navajo and Wintu and Chinese (see my essay "Language and the World"), all the base words can be used in compounds: there simply is no division of words into nouns, adjectives, verbs, and adverbs.

Appendix C Negation in Mass-Process Languages

Dorothy Lee in "Conceptual Implications of an Indian Language" says that the Wintu do not have "not" as a propositional negator:

> To express negative obligation the *-les* is affixed to the negative auxiliary *ele(u)* which means *to not (do)*, *to not (be)*. p. 133

> I translate *eleu* as *to not-do* or *to not-be*; actually, it means: *to not*.
> It is not a negative statement, but rather, a positive assertion of negation. p. 131n

Compare our use of "refrain from" in English as discussed in my essay "Reasoning with Prescriptive Claims".

Jürgen Broschart in "Why Tongan Does It Differently: Categorial Distinctions in a Language without Nouns and Verbs", says:

> In Tongan, '*ikai* '(be) not' is a predicate of its own ('it is not that . . .', see example [43]) and does not help to differentiate the entities in question. p. 161

> 43   oku 'ikai ke   pule'anga
>   PRES NOT   SUBJUNCT   government
>   'It does not belong to the government.' (lit. 'It is not that it government-s.')   p. 145

Compare how we differentiate between propositional negation and predicate negation in English. There are two readings of "Birta is not a cat". The first is to take "not" to attach to the predicate: "Birta is not-(a cat)". For this to be true, Birta must exist: she has some "property", namely not being a cat. The other reading is to take "not" to apply to the proposition: "not: Birta is a cat". This could be true if Birta does not exist.[1]

Mark Donohue, Bhojraj Gautam, and Madhav Pokharel in "Negation and Nominalization in Kusunda" give an example that shows how easy it is project the grammatical categories of one's own language onto another.

> Sentences that are offered as translation of negative sentences in Nepali are easily elicited in Kusunda, as in Example 2. Given the Nepali prompt in 2a, the Kusunda translation in 2b is readily forthcoming.
>
> (2) a. Nepali
>   Maile makai kha-i-na.
>   1SG.ERG corn eat-1Sg.PST-NEG
>
>   b. Kusunda
>   Tsi ipə n t-ə m-u
>   1SG corn I-eat-'NEG'
>
> The problem is that the sentence in 2b can also be elicited by asking for a translation of 'I will eat corn', 'I don't want to eat corn', 'I won't eat corn', and various other possible prompts. This is because the suffix *-u*, rather than marking the negative, in fact marks a more general irrealis, which includes among its functions 'negation' as part of the general unrealized category.   p. 738

---

[1] See *The Internal Structure of Predicates and Names*.

Appendix D Strawson on Mass Terms and Individuals

In his book *Individuals*, P. F. Strawson discusses mass terms and how to think of them in relation to our talk of individuals.

> I have in mind what I shall call *feature-universals* or *feature-concepts,* and what I shall call *feature-placing statements*. As examples, I suggest the following:
>
> > Now it is raining.
> > Snow is falling.
> > There is coal here.
> > There is gold here.
> > There is water here.
>
> The universal terms introduced into these propositions do not function as characterizing universals. *Snow, water, coal* and *gold,* for example, are general kinds of stuff, not properties or characteristics of particulars; though *being made of snow* or *being made of gold* are characteristics of particulars. Nor are the universal terms introduced into these propositions sortal universals. No one of them of itself provides a principle of distinguishing, enumerating and reidentifying particulars of a sort. But each can be very easily modified so as to yield several such principles: we can distinguish, count and reidentify *veins* or *grains, lumps* or *dumps* of coal, and *flakes, falls, drifts* or *expanses* of snow. Such phrases as 'lump of coal' or 'fall of snow' introduce sortal universals; but 'coal' and 'snow' *simpliciter* do not. These sentences, then, neither contain any part which introduces a particular, nor any expression used in such a way that its use presupposes the use of expressions to introduce particulars. Of course, when these sentences are used, the combination of the circumstances of their use with the tense of the verb and the demonstrative adverbs, if any, which they contain, yields a statement of the incidence of the universal feature they introduce. For this much at least is essential to any language in which singular empirical statements could be made at all: viz. the introduction of general concepts and the indication of their incidence. But it is an important fact that this can be done by means of statements which neither bring particulars into our discourse nor presuppose other areas of discourse in which particulars are brought in.
>
> Languages imagined on the model of such languages as these are sometimes called 'property-location' languages. But this is an unfortunate name: the universal terms which figure in my examples are not properties; indeed, the idea of a property belongs to a level of complexity which we are trying to get below. This is why I have chosen to use the less philosophically committed word 'feature', and to speak of 'feature-placing' sentences.
>
> pp. 202–203

Note that Strawson does not consider beauty or justice. Are these feature-placing? As soon as we ask that, we see that Strawson has introduced a major metaphysics here, for he says he is talking about "feature universals" or "feature concepts", where in my work I talk about the words "beauty" and "justice". We can say "Beauty here now" and "Justice there then". Perhaps Strawson would say that "justice" and "beauty" are not "really" features, not really masses. But why? It has to be, I think, because "justice" and "beauty" aren't substances. But then why is it that we can assert "That is an instance of justice"?

Isn't that instance a part of the world? How is it different from objects and masses? We can't evade this issue by invoking events, as I explain in "Why Event-Talk Is a Problem".

What does Strawson mean by "a statement of the incidence of the universal feature"? Perhaps that is what I call "description in a context".

Strawson continues:

> Though feature-placing sentences do not introduce particulars into our discourse, they provide a basis for this introduction. The facts they state are presupposed, in the required sense, by the introduction of certain kinds of particular. That there should be facts statable by means of such sentences as 'There is water here', 'It is snowing', is a condition of there being propositions into which particulars are introduced by means of such expressions as 'This pool of water;' 'This fall of snow'. In general, the transition from facts of the presupposed kind to the introduction of the particulars for which they supply the basis involves a conceptual complication: it involves the adoption of criteria of distinctness and, where applicable, criteria of reidentification for particulars of the kind in question, as well as the use of characterizing universals which can be tied to a particular of that kind. A *basis* for criteria of distinctness may indeed already exist at the feature-placing level. For where we can say 'There is snow here' or 'There is gold here', we can also, perhaps, say, 'There is snow (gold) *here*—and *here*—and *here*.' Factors which determine multiplicity of placing may become, when we introduce particulars, criteria for distinguishing one particular from another.　　pp. 203–204

Chapter 7 of his book is titled "Language without Particulars". This sounds like what we're doing here. But he doesn't go with a language without particulars. He introduces times and places, and with those as things he says that you can get particulars. He talks about identifying a place by an object that is exactly in it: "Suppose there were a block of granite which maintained its position and its boundaries unchanged." (p. 223) But as I show in *Time and Space in Formal Logic* (pp. 179–181) this is a fantasy and not a method of identification.

Appendix E Talk of Time in the Flow of All

Context with before and after

Time is mass in our common conception, though some mathematicians and philosophers say it is composed of dimensionless instants. But what those instants are and how they can together compose an interval of time—this they cannot say.

Time is process, a flow, always flowing. In our common conception we say it flows from the past through the present to the future. But what the flow is and how we can grasp the ever-flowing present, no one seems to be able to say.

Do we experience time? All we can say with some confidence is that we experience before and after, ascribing or sensing this before that. What is the "this" and "that"? Perhaps those are indescribable, only in our sensing. But when we want to communicate we describe: "Spot barked", "Dick yelled", "SPOT + BARK", "DICK + YELL".

We note or impose order on our experience saying this is a correct description before that. "SPOT + BARK" is a correct description before "DICK + YELL" is a correct description. But that is to say wrong. Better is to say that the descriptions themselves are not ordered but what they describe—in the flow of all—is ordered. "SPOT + BARK" describes correctly of the flow of all before "DICK + YELL" describes correctly of the flow of all. But again that is wrong, for it makes it sound as if we are comparing when those words were asserted. Saying anything in the world as the flow of all taking account of time is likely to lead us thing-language talkers into assumptions and conceptions of time as times or of some part of the world that we can pick out or imagine ourselves picking out.

Simply we can say:

(1)   SPOT + BARK <u>before</u> DICK + YELL

We can use "<u>before</u>" as a categorematic linking, assuming or hoping that we understand it well enough to talk together. We have "<u>after</u>" by reversing the words: "DICK + YELL <u>after</u> SPOT + BARK" is a correct description iff (1) is correct.

We can specify a context as some of the flow of all in which we note before and after by linking correct descriptions with "<u>before</u>". That is, a scenario includes evaluating categorematic words linked by "<u>before</u>". Compare: Wanda is standing in line to buy a ticket to a concert. She has a place in the queue. The context is not that place where she is standing but that place in the queue.

But there are problems using this way to talk of the flow of all. Consider:

(2)   Spot barked. Then Dick yelled. Then Spot barked.

It's clear to us that the second "Spot barked" is meant to describe after Dick yelled, while the first is meant to describe before Dick yelled. They are not equivalent. We know this without reflection when we speak English. Interpreting (2) in talk of the flow of all, not concerned yet with the past tense, we have:

(SPOT + BARK <u>before</u> DICK + YELL)

∧ (DICK + YELL <u>before</u> SPOT + BARK)

We have to distinguish the two occurrences of "SPOT + BARK". Suppose we use subscripts:

138   Appendix E

(3)   ((SPOT + BARK)$_1$ <u>before</u> (DICK + YELL))

       ∧ ((DICK + YELL) <u>before</u> (SPOT + BARK)$_2$)

How do we know which indexed version of a word is meant to describe before or after another? We can do that only by invoking that one is meant to describe before the other. And that is circular. Perhaps we could expand the descriptions in some way, but I can't see how any more than how we could expand the descriptions "Spot barked" in (2). All we have is before and after. Worse, we'd need to do this with each word we use, including "DICK + YELL", so instead of (3) we'd have:

(4)   ((SPOT + BARK)$_1$ <u>before</u> (DICK + YELL)$_{17}$)

       ∧ ((DICK + YELL)$_{17}$ <u>before</u> SPOT + BARK)$_2$)

Additionally, we'd have to find a way to say that if "(SPOT + BARK)$_1$" is a correct description in the context established in (4), then both "SPOT" and "BARK" are correct descriptions in that context. But those, too, have to be indexed. Which indices to use and how to ensure that there are indexed versions of "SPOT" and "BARK" that overlap from before and after "(SPOT + BARK)$_1$" is a problem. The complications multiply.

It's not impossible. I've worked out a system along these lines using as a guide logics for taking account of before and after reasoning about the world as made up of things from *Time and Space in Formal Logic*. But reviewing that work, trying to make it clearer, I couldn't make good sense of how to understand and use the system. Though I had overcome the technical problems I had not resolved the conceptual ones. Perhaps someone else will be more successful.

Time and location for context

Perhaps we can specify context in terms of time and location, as we did in many examples.

Instead of taking "CRL" as a context word for the corral last night, we might take "<u>CR</u>" for the location of the corral and "<u>LN</u>" for last night. But aren't those too vague to use? What is the location of the corral? Shall we assume that the wire mesh fence, with all its wobbles and leaning fence posts, delimits a particular part of . . . what? Of space? And what of the ground below and space above? Shall we assume that last night was December 20, 2009, beginning at . . . sunset? at last light? The location-word "<u>CR</u>" and the time-word "<u>LN</u>" are not meant to pick out some of the flow of all any more than "RUN" as a correct description picks out some clearly delineated part of the flow of all. These words describe in the flow of all, though pointing, indicating how we are to use these words, is still essential for our talk. They need be no more precise than descriptions of context we've been using.

So we can say:

(1)   SHEEP (<<u>LN</u>, <u>CR</u>>)

By this we mean that we take the pair of words <<u>LN</u>, <u>CR</u>> to establish context. Then (1) is correct or it is not correct.

If we take a time-word and location-word pair to establish a context, then for a pair <$\underline{T}$, $\underline{L}$> to describe a context that is within <$\underline{T}$´, $\underline{L}$´> we need that both $\underline{T}$ is within $\underline{T}$´ and $\underline{L}$ is within $\underline{L}$´. That seems straighforward, except that we talk of the location of a video conference. Is a URL a location? We can view a meeting on the internet as a context, but as a location? What would be a location within that location? There are many other examples of context we've seen that are difficult if not impossible to understand in terms of time and location.

I invite others to investigate how we might specify context with time-words and location-words. Introducing categorematic connectives "<u>before</u>", "<u>within</u>" seem needed, but unclear in application. Worse, talk of times and locations leads to thinking of those as things, which is not compatible with our view of the world as the flow of all.

Appendix F   Expanding Our Talk in the Flow of All?

Context less context

Suppose I want to tell you that there is sheep-ing now in the part of the corral which doesn't include the shed. I can't use "SHEEP [CRL] ∧ (¬ SHEEP [SHD])" because for this to be correct there must be no sheep-ing in SHD, yet all I mean is that there is sheep-ing in a part of the context CRL, the part that doesn't include SHD. I can't use "CRL + (non-SHD)" because "+" and "non-" are for combining categorematic words via their concepts, and a context word is not meant to elicit a concept. How can I direct your attention to CRL except for SHD? I can assert:

   SHEEP [CRL ~ SHD]

This is meant to evaluate "SHEEP" in CRL not in SHD. Similarly, I can assert:

   CAT [SCR ~ DGS]

There is cat-ing in context SCR that is not in DGS. And I can assert that there is dog-ing in PTO but not in CRL with:

   DOG [PTO ~ CRL]

Since CRL does not overlap PTO, this is correct iff "SHEEP [PTO]" is correct.

A word for a context except for a part   If W and V stand for context words then (W ~ V) is a context word meant to stand for: context W except for context V. We pronounce it as "W except for V".

If V does not overlap W, then (W ~ V) stands for context W.

This definition allows for repeating this way of making a context word. For example, let "TR" stand for the area in the corral at Dogshine that is under the large tree eight paces from the shed. Then we can form:

   ((CRL ~ SHD) ~ TR)

This stands for context the corral last night except for context of the shed, and then except for context of the area under the large tree. Compare this with:

   (CRL ~ (SHD ~ TR))

Since TR does not overlap SHD, this is another way to establish CRL ~ SHD as context.

Overlap of context

We might also devise a way to talk of overlapping of contexts. Let "BF" be a context word for on the feeder when the picture on the left was taken, and let "BBF" be a context word for the area below the feeder at that time.

Then I could direct your attention to the overlap of these contexts with:

BF ∩ BBF

Generally we could use for context "the" overlap of context specified by context word W and context specified by context word V:

(W ∩ V)

But if there's no overlap, then (W ∩ V) doesn't establish a context, and we said we wouldn't allow that.

This seems to be an adaptation of the methods of set-theory: intersection, union, complement, which are so dependent on a thing-view of the world that I've not developed it.

Context within context

In evaluating whether a categorematic word is correct relative to a context, we rely on understanding whether a context is within another context and whether a context overlaps another context. Perhaps we can bring that analysis into our talk in the flow of all. For any context words W and U, we could adopt as words:

W within U

W overlap U

Each would be correct or incorrect, with no talk of concept, for they link context words. With these we could state some principles:

Correct within a context, then correct in the context

((E)[W] ∧ (W within U)) ⊃ (E)[U]

No overlap then correct in W ~ U iff correct in W

((E)[W ~ U] ∧ ¬(W overlap U)) ⊃ (E)[W]

We could give principles in our talk of the flow of all governing these linkings:

W within W

((W within X) ∧ (X within Y)) ⊃ (W within Y)

W overlap W

(W overlap U) ⊃ (U overlap W)

If we adopt these new kind of linkings and words, we should expand our system of reasoning to allow derivations from them. But these simple forms conceal a problem in interpretation. Does the context of Socorro today overlap the context of Socorro two days ago? Not in time, but yes in space. Does CRL ~ (SHD) overlap SHD? Not in location, but yes in time.

Schemes of inferences marked with more than one context

We can consider schemes of inferences marked for more than one context.

(1) SHEEP [SHD]
     Therefore, SHEEP [CRL]

Knowing the contexts that "SHD" and "CRL" stand for, we can see that the premise is correct and conclusion is correct. But that's not an inference. What we would be concerned with is:

SHEEP [W]
Therefore, SHEEP [U]

But for this to be a generalization of (1) it needs a further premise that we know is correct for (1):

SHEEP [W]
W <u>within</u> U
Therefore, SHEEP [U]

This project would need to be developed along with using "<u>within</u>" and "<u>overlap</u>" as linkings of context words.

Different ways to interpret
Consider:

(2) In the patio Arf heard Birta barking in the corral.

Here are some ways we could interpret this.

a. With no talk of context
If context is specified only outside our talk in the flow of all, we can interpret this as:

(3) ((ARF + HEAR) <u>in</u> (PATIO)) directed towards

((BIRTA + BARK) <u>in</u> (CORRAL))

To assert this, we need to specify a context to be evaluate it. Suppose it's my ranch Dogshine this morning. Then (3) is correct. If the context were New York, it would be incorrect.

b. Specifying a context in talk of the flow of all
If we take "DGST" for context Dogshine this morning, we can interpret (2) as:

(4) (((ARF + HEAR) <u>in</u> (PATIO)) directed towards

((BIRTA + BARK) <u>in</u> (CORRAL))) [DGST]

This is correct; no further specification of context needed.

c. Using local categorematic words
We can interpret (2) as:

(5) [[(ARF + HEAR) [PTO]]] directed towards [[(BIRTA + BARK) [CORL]]]

To assert this we need to specify a context. Taking that to be DGST, we have:

[[(ARF + HEAR) [PTO]]] directed towards [[(BIRTA + BARK) [CORL]]] [DGST]

Yet in (3) don't we already have specifications of context? Compare:

(ARF + HEAR) <u>in</u> (PATIO)

(ARF + HEAR) [PTO]

The first could be correct in the context of Dogshine this morning but not correct in the context of New Zealand today. It only seems to have an indication of context with "in PATIO". The second needs no further context to be correct or incorrect.

Quantity
Dick said to Zoe:

> There was more snow here in the yard yesterday than today.

We don't have ways to talk of how much snow. Both "a little" and "much" are too vague, though we use them in our ordinary speech. But comparing quantities is not too vague.

We have "DZY" as a context word for Dick and Zoe's yard today, and we can take "DZYY" as context word for Dick and Zoe's yard yesterday. Then we can form the local categorematic words "[[SNOW [DZY]]] " and "[[SNOW [DZYY]]] " and make a comparison by using a new categorematic connective "more than":

(6) [[SNOW [DZY]]] more than [[SNOW [DZYY]]]

To interpret what Dick said as an assertion, we note that he's talking in DZY and use that as the context for (6):

> ([[SNOW [DZY]]] more than [[SNOW [DZYY]]]) [DZY]

With principles governing this connective we could make comparisons of quantity, though it's not clear how we would evaluate

Bibliography

- Only works cited in the text or elsewhere in the bibliography are listed.
- Citations are to the most recent English reference listed unless noted otherwise.
- Works cited in the text without attribution are by Richard L. Epstein.

AXELROD, Melissa
    1993   *The Semantics of Time: Aspectual Categorization in Koyukon Athabascan*
              University of Nebraska Press.

BROSCHART, Jürgen
    1997   Why Tongan Does It Differently: Categorial Distinctions in a Language without Nouns and Verbs
              Linguistic Typology, vol. 1, pp. 123–165.

BUNT, Harry C.
    1985   *Mass Terms and Model Theoretic Semantics*
              Cambridge University Press.

DONOHUE, Mark, Bhojraj GAUTAM, and Madhav POKHAREL
    2014   Negation and Nominalization in Kusunda
              Language, vol. 90, no. 3, pp. 737–745.

EPSTEIN, Richard L.
    1990   *Propositional Logics*
              Kluwer. 3rd edition, Advanced Reasoning Forum, 2012.
    1994   *Predicate Logic*
              Oxford University Press. Reprinted Advanced Reasoning Forum, 2012.
    2011   *Cause and Effect, Conditionals, Explanations*
              (*Essays on Logic as the Art of Reasoning Well*)
              Advanced Reasoning Forum.
    2011A   Conditionals
              In EPSTEIN 2011.
    2012   *Reasoning in Science and Mathematics*
              (*Essays on Logic as the Art of Reasoning Well*)
              Advanced Reasoning Forum.
    2012A   Models and Theories
              In EPSTEIN 2012, pp. 19–51.
    2013A   *The Fundamentals of Argument Analysis*
              (*Essays on Logic as the Art of Reasoning Well*)
              Advanced Reasoning Forum.
    2013B   Subjective Claims
              with Fred Kroon and William S. Robinson.
              In EPSTEIN 2013A, pp. 95–127.
    2013C   *Prescriptive Reasoning*
              (*Essays on Logic as the Art of Reasoning Well*)
              Advanced Reasoning Forum.
    2013D   Reasoning with Prescriptive Claims
              In EPSTEIN 2013C, pp. 1–95.

> 2014 *Conventional Gestures: Meaning and Methodology*
> Advanced Reasoning Forum.
> 2015 *Reasoning and Formal Logic*
> (*Essays on Logic as the Art of Reasoning Well*)
> Advanced Reasoning Forum.
> 2015A Truth and Reasoning
> In EPSTEIN, 2015, pp. 57–83.
> 2015B On the Error in Frege's Proof that Names Denote
> In EPSTEIN, 2015, pp. 150–155.
> 2016 *The Internal Structure of Predicates and Names*
> Advanced Reasoning Forum.
> 2021 *Language and the World: Essays New and Old*
> Advanced Reasoning Forum.
> 2021A Language-Thought-Meaning
> In EPSTEIN, 2021, pp. 60–85.
> 2022 *Time and Space in Formal Logic*
> Advanced Reasoning Forum.
> 2022 Is There A Problem with Formal Semantics for Natural Languages?
> Available at <www.AdvancedReasoningForum.org>.

FULLER, B.A.G. and Sterling M. McMURRIN
> 1955 *A History of Philosophy*
> 3rd edition, Henry Holt and Company.

GIRJU, Roxana, Dan MOLDOVAN, Marta TATU, and Daniel ANTOHE
> 2005 On the Semantics of Noun Compounds
> *Computer Speech and Language*, Volume 19, pp. 479–496.

HANSEN, Chad
> 1983 *Language and Logic in Ancient China*
> The Univ. of Michigan Press. Reprinted 2020, Advanced Reasoning Forum.
> 1985 Individualism in Chinese Thought
> In *Individualism and Holism: Studies in Confucian and Taoist Values*, ed. Donald Munro, University of Michigan Center for Chinese Studies, 1985, pp. 35–56.

HANSON, Norwood Russell
> 1958 *Patterns of Discovery*
> Cambridge University Press.

KELLER, Helen
> 1903 *The Story of My Life*
> The Century Company.

LEE, Dorothy Demetracopoulou
> 1938 Conceptual Implications of an Indian Language
> *Philosophy of Science*, vol. 5, no. 1, 1938, pp. 89–102.
> Reprinted in EPSTEIN, 2021, pp. 124–138.
> 1944 Categories of the Generic and the Particular in Wintu"
> *American Anthropologist*, vol. 46, no. 3, 1944, pp. 362–369.
> Reprinted in EPSTEIN, 2021, pp. 139–147.

LEVINSON, Stephen C.
    1996   Relativity in Spatial Conception and Description
              In *Rethinking Linguistic Relativity*, eds. John J. Gomperz and
              Stephen C. Levinson, Cambridge University Press, pp. 177–202.

MATES, Benson
    1996   *The Skeptic Way: Sextus Empiricus's* Outlines of Pyrrhonism
              Oxford University Press.

PELLETIER, Francis Jeffrey and Lenhart K. SCHUBERT
    1989   Mass expressions
              Chapter IV.4 of *Handbook of Philosophical Logic, Volume 4: Topics in the
              Philosophy of Language*, eds. D. Gabbay and F. Guenthner, D. Reidel.

QUINE, Willard van Orman
    1953   On What There Is
              In Quine, *From a Logical Point of View*, Harvard University Press,
              2nd ed., 1961, pp. 1–19.
    1960   *Word and Object*
              The M.I.T. Press.

STRAWSON, P. F.
    1959   *Individuals: An Essay in Descriptive Metaphysics*
              Routledge.

TOUGH, Joan
    1977   *The Development of Meaning*
              George Allen & Unwin.

WAISMANN, Friedrich
    1945   Verifiability
              Proceedings of the Aristotelian Society, Supp. Vol. 19, 1945, pp. 119–150.
              Reprinted in *The Theory of Meaning*, ed. G.H.R. Parkinson, Oxford
              University Press, 1968, pp. 33–60.

Context Words

in the order presented in the chapters

PTO	the patio at Dogshine this morning
CRL	the corral at Arf's ranch last night
CORL	the corral at Arf's ranch
SHD	the shed in the corral at Dogshine
DGS	Arf's ranch Dogshine
SCR	Socorro County, New Mexico
NZ	New Zealand
UNIC	all places and times in the world as we know it in which "UNICORN" is correct
BH	behind the bale of hay in SHD
SCRM	Socorro County this morning
GNID	July 6, 2024, in Luis Lopez, New Mexico
GSN	general context of where we are discussing rats
WRLD	the world as it is, was, and will be
DZY	Dick and Zoe's yard today
CRLM	CRL this morning
DZYA	Dick and Zoe's yard three years ago
FN	where Zoe is speaking in the forest now
FY	where Zoe is speaking now in the forest yesterday
RFRG	in the refrigerator a few minutes ago
GLS	in the glass now
KS	when and where Kim spilled coffee
SW	when and where Sandy wiped up coffee
DS	where Dick is now speaking
UB	where the mud was previously
DZTW	where Dick, Zoe, and Tom are talking
YIK	where one patch of mud is
ZIK	where another patch of mud is
PRK	15 years ago in a park when Shondel and Zoe's mother were and the only female child in the park at that time was Zoe

Index of Examples

Listed here are examples in the example-analysis format or for which there is a substantial discussion in the text.

Blanks come before all other letters and symbols. Quotation marks " " are treated as blanks. Symbols come after letters in the ordering. Order of symbols: / + − ¬ ∧ ∨ •> . Entirely formal (schematic) examples are at the end.

A dog house that's made to look like a castle. 20
All is change. 117
"(ARFITO)" ≈ "(ARFITO)" 58
"((ARF + WALK) with (ARFITO + BARK))"
    ≈ "((ARFITO + BARK) with (ARF + WALK))" 59

BEAUTY 15
"(BLACK − GREY − WHITE − CLEAR)" ≡ "(non-(COLOR))"
    "(BLACK − GREY − WHITE − CLEAR)" ≠ "(non-(COLOR))" 59
Birta is a dog. 94
Birta is barking. 94
Birta is brown. Therefore, something is brown. 95

Cartoon cat. 18
CAT − (non-DOG) 42
CAT − ((non-DOG) / HOUSE) 33
CAT + ((non-DOG) / HOUSE) 33
CAT ∨ ((non-DOG) / HOUSE) 44
(CAT) ∨ ¬ (DOG) 67
Cat-ing is evil-ing. 97
Competent teaching. 19

Dick asks Zoe why she's screwing up her nose. She says she smells the same skunk odor that was here yesterday. 115
Dick had the same idea as Suzy. 117
Dick's mind is not the same as Dick's body. 118
(DOG inside FENCE) therefore (DOG) 67
(DOG) therefore (DOG inside FENCE) 67
"(DEAD)" ≢ "(non-(ALIVE))"
    "(DEAD)" ≠ "(non-(ALIVE))" 59
DOG + CAT 24
(DOG + BARK + CHASE) therefore (CAT) 67
DOG + (non-GREYHOUND) 31
"(DOG + RUN)" ≈ "(DOG + DOG + RUN)" 58
DOG − CAT 43
DOG (non-DOG) 32

Index of Examples

"((DOG/RUN) + (RED/APPLE))" ≈ "((RED/APPLE) + (DOG/RUN))" 62
(DOG) ∨ ¬ (DOG) 67
Every rat is brown. 95

F therefore E 68
(F + G + H) therefore E 67
Fake dog. 18
FAKE / DOG
    DOG / FAKE 25
For any categorematic words E, F, G, H, •> (E + F) – (G + H) ≈ (G + H) – (F + E) 62

(GRASS + GREEN) ∧ ¬ (GRASS + GREEN)
    (GRASS + GREEN) ∧ (GRASS + non-GREEN) 43
GURGLE 34

HORSE + DONKEY 24
"(HORSE – BROWN)" ≈ "(BROWN – HORSE)" 57
"((HOUSE with CAR) – ((DOG + (non-BARK)))" ≈
    "(((DOG + (non-BARK)) – (HOUSE withCAR))" 62
HOUSE / (non-DOG) 32
"(HOUSE / SIBLING)" ≈ "(HOUSE / (BROTHER – SISTER))" 58

If " (FORGET)" ≈ "non-(REMEMBER)" is one of the initial particular equivalences, then
    •> "(DOG + FORGET)" ≈ "(non-(REMEMBER) + DOG)". 63
If "(PUP)" ≈ "(POOCH)", and "((POOCH)" ≈ "(DOG)", then "(PUP)" ≈ "(DOG)". 59
If "(PUP) ≈ (POOCH)", then "(POOCH) ≈ (PUP)". 59
If "(SIBLING)" ≈ "(SISTER–BROTHER)" is one of the initial particular equivalences, then:
    •> "(HOUSE / SIBLING)" ≈ (HOUSE / (SISTER–BROTHER))". 63
If we take some ice cubes from the refrigerator, crush them, and put them into a glass of coke,
    we may say: The ice in the coke is the same ice that was in the refrigerator before. 115
Imaginary dog. 19
It's raining. 3, 93
It's not raining. 93
It was raining. 93

JUSTICE + HUMAN 23

Leucippus ... proclaimed that empty space—or the void—exists 96

(non-BROWN)
    ¬ (BROWN) 41
non-DOG 31
(non-DOG) directed towards CAT
    ¬ (DOG directed towards CAT) 42
non-(DOG + CAT)
    ¬ (DOG + CAT) 41
(non-DOG) / HOUSE 32

(non-GREEN)
    ¬ (GREEN) 41
non–(non–TOY) 32
not •> (E $\underline{c}$ F ≈ F $\underline{c}$ E)
not •> ((E + F) ≈ E) 63

PARROT + (non-GREEN)
    ¬ (PARROT + GREEN) 41
pigs can fly 71

SIBLING 59
"(SIBLING)" ≈ "(BROTHER – SISTER)" 58, 63
Snow is white. 97
Some rats are brown and some rats are not brown. 95
STORY / PEGASUS 19
SWEET + SOUR 24
Swimming is fun. 97

The paint there is drying. 96
The paint there is wet. 96
The river is very deep here. Don't step into it. 117
The water in the pond in my patio is part of all water. 116
There are two patches of mud now in the patio. 118
This dog existed here three years ago. 115
This is the same cold we had before. 118
This mud used to be brown. 116
This running used to be fast. 117
Tomato seeds. Bird seeds. 24
Toy bears and bear toys. 18
TOY / (DOG + RUN) 25
"(TOY / (DOG – WOLF))" ≈ "(TOY / (WOLF – DOG))" 58
TOY / (non-DOG) 31
TOY / UNICORN 19

Um ser superior cuida de nos. 93
Unicorns don't exist. 95

WIND + LEAF 24
With context a patch of mud in my patio, in any context within that,
    "MUD" is a correct description iff "BROWN" is a correct description. 59

¬ (DOG + CHASE <u>directed towards</u> CAT) 42
¬ (DOG ∧ (¬ BARK)) 43
¬ (E $\underline{c}$ G) ∧ ¬ (F $\underline{d}$ H) therefore ¬ ((E $\underline{c}$ G) – (F $\underline{d}$ H)) 68
¬ (HORSE – DONKEY) 42
¬ (¬ (CAT)) 42

Index of Examples

¬ (¬ (CAT ∧ ¬ DOG)) 42
¬ ((¬ DOG) ∧ (¬ CAT)) 42

•> "(CAT + RUN + BLACK)" ≈ "(BLACK + CAT + RUN)" 63
•> "(DOG+BARK)" ≈ "(DOG+BARK)" 62
•> "(RUN ≈ RUN)" 62

(A ∧ B) ∧ ¬ C   100

E [W] 101

E [W] ∧ F [U] 101

E [W] ∧ F [W] 101

(E [W] ∧ F [W]) ⊃ G [U]
   (E [W] ∧ F [W]) ⊃ G [W]   101

((E + F) / G)
   ((¬ (F − G)) ∧ (G/H))
   ((F ⊆ E) − (G + H))   100

(E + F) [W] 102

(E + F) [W]
   (G ⊆ H) [W] ⊃ (E[W]) 102

(E + F) [W] ∧ (G − (H[W])) [W] 101

(E + F) [W] ∧ (G − H) [W]
   (E ⊆ F) [U] ∧ ¬ ((G − H) [U]) 101

Index of Symbols

in the order they appear in the text
"iff" abbreviates "if and only if"

-ing 8, 10

/ 17

+ 21

directed towards 27

c̱ 28

− 29–30

non- 31

¬ 38–39

∧ 39

∨ 43

⊃ 44

E, F, ..., H, K 23, 57, 80, 106

E, F, G, H, W, Y 61

A, B, C, D 47, 80

≈ 57

≉ 57

≡ 57

≢ 57

DCE 61

•> 61

therefore 66

R, S, T, bold-face
   capital letters 72, 105

A, B, ... ⊨$_S$ C 72, 105

A, B, ... ⊨ C 72, 106

⊨$_S$ A 72, 106

⊨ A 72, 106

⊭ 72, 106

⊢ A 81, 108

⊬ A 81, 108

A, B, C, ... ⊢ D 84, 109

E [W] 91

[[E [W]]] 111

Index

Underlined page numbers indicate a definition, statement of principle, or quotation.

abstractions, 97
adjectives, 5, Chap 5 (15–16), 131–133
adverbs, 5, Chap 5 (15–16)
agreements, 13, 14
   subjectivity and —, 13
"almost", 20
Antohe, Daniel, 132–133
appears in, 46–47
assertion, 9, 34
   categorematic word marked for
      context is —, 89
   is local —, 34
attention. *See* paying attention.
Axelrod, Melissa, 130

base word, 8–9
   valid?, 73
before and after, 137–138
Broschart, Jürgen, 134
Bunt, Harry C., 115–116, 123–124

categorematic linking, Chap 8 (26–28)
categorematic word(s), 8–9
   base —. *See* base word.
   complex. *See* complex categorematic
      word(s).
   compound words compared to —, 38–39,
      Chap 12 (41–44)
   context words different from —, 88
   correct in context, 9
   elicits a concept, 8–9
   evaluated locally, 32, 34
   local —. *See* local categorematic word(s).
   marked for context, 89–90, 91
      is an assertion, 89
   three roles of —, 34
   used as modifier, Chap 6 (17–20)
   used to describe in context, 9–11, 51
change, 2-3, 112–113, 116, 117
Chinese, 5, 8, 12, 133
classifier, 122–124
color words, 15, Appx A (128–130)
compatible instantiations, 49–50, 100

complex categorematic word(s), 20, 34, 46
   base word elicits same concept as —?, 58
   concept elicited by —, 51
   forms of —, 46
   marked for context, 90
      forms of —, 99
   valid due to its form?, 74–75
compound nouns, Appx B (131–133)
compound word(s), Chap 11 (38–40)
   categorematic words compared to —, 38–39,
      Chap 12 (41–44)
   derivations of —, 81–82, 86, 108
   marked for context, 90, 99
      derivations of —, 108
compound word scheme, 47
   initial —, 81
concept(s), 8, Chap 4 (13–14)
   determines whether word is correct, 14
   elicited by categorematic word, 8–9, 51
   not reducible to correct assertions, 13–14
conceptual equivalence, Chap 15 (56–60), 57
   deriving —, Chap 16 (61–64)
   initial schemes for deriving —, 61
   relative to a scenario?, 78–79
   substitution of —, 58
   transitivity of, 59, 61
   yields descriptive equivalence, 57, 82
conclusion, 66
   scheme, 67
conjunction, 39–40
connective,
   global, local, 46, 99
consequence, 66
context(s), 9–10
   all (every) —, 10, 89, 94–95
   establishing —, 10
   in English, 12
   general —, 71
   — less context, 140
   overlap of —, 140–141
   paying attention and —, 10, 89
   restricting to — in which E is correct, 74
   scenarios clarify —, 69–71

context (continued)
    some —, 10
    some of —, 31, 34
    within context, talk of, 141
context word(s), Chap 21 (88–103)
    categorematic words different from —, 88
continuity, 2–3, 11
correct description, 9, 51–52
    is of some of context, 31, 34
    marked categorematic word is —, 103
    not — is default judgment, 33
counting, 117

DCE, 61
denying, 39
derivability of inferences reduced
    to derivability of words, 84, 109
derivable inference is valid, 84, 109
derivable word is valid, 81, 108
derivation,
    in **IXN**, 80–81
    in **WMC**, 107–108
    of conceptual equivalences, 61
    of inference, 84
        marked for context, 109
        reduced to derivation of words, 84
    of valid compound word schemes, 82, 86
    of word, 81–82
        marked for context, 109
    reasoning and —, 86
describing, 10
    all, 4
    not partitioning, 5, 10
description,
    correct —, 9, 51–52, 136
    global —, 38–39
    local —, 34
    not correct is default judgment, 33
    of some of context, 31, 34
descriptive equivalence, Chap 15 (56–60),
    57, Chap 16 (61–64)
    of local categorematic words, 113
    substitution and —, 58
disjoining categorematic words, Chap 9 (29–30)
    disjunction compared to —, 43
    order of words doesn't matter in —, 30
    redundancy in —, 30
disjunction, 43

Donohue, Mark, 134

evil, 97–98
existence, 4, 19, 89, 93–94, 95, 96–97, 115,
    128, 134
experience, 2–4, 12, 13–14, 66, 79, 93, 114
    same —?, 129–130
    time and —, 137

facts, 128, 130
feature-placing sentences, 135–136
fiction talk, 19
flow of all, 5
    part of —, 9
formal language, 50
formalizing ordinary language?, 93
forms of words, Chap 13 (46–50),
    Chap 23 (99–102)
flux, 2–4
Fuller, B.A.G., 96

Gautam, Bhoraj, 134
general context, 71, 94
gestures, 38
Girju, Roxana, 132–133
global connectives, 46
global negation, 39
God, 94

Hansen, Chad, 12, 124
Hanson, Norwood Russell, 128
Heraclitus, 117
hook, 44

I, 2
identity, 113–114
iff = if and only if
incorrect description as default judgment, 33
    See also correct description; null words.
inference(s), Chap 7 (66–68), 66
    derivable reduced to derivable words, 84, 109
    derivable — is valid, 84
    deriving in **IXN**, 84
    invalid —, 66
    marked for context, 104–105
    marked for single context, 105
    open —, 105
    scheme of, 67

inference(s) (continued)
    valid —, 66
        in scenario, 71
        reduced to validity of words, 84, 109
infinitely many premises ?, 86
-ing, 8, 10
initial schemes for deriving,
    conceptual equivalences, 61
    valid words, 80
        marked for context, 107–108
        with local words, 120
instance of a scheme, 47, 100
    open —, 100
instantiation(s) of a scheme, 47
    compatible —, 49–50, 99–100
intersubjectivity, 13, 125
IXN, 81

javelina, 13–14
Juney, 2

Keller, Helen, 14
Koyukon, 130
Kroon, Fred, 124
Kusunda, 134

Lee, Dorothy, 123, 134
Leucippus, 96
Levinson, Stephen C., 28, 133
linking categorematic words, Chap 8 (26–28)
local categorematic word(s), Chap 27
        (110–114), 111, 120
    elicit concepts, 110–111, 120
    initial principles for —, 120
    mistaken —, 111
local connective, 46, 99
location, 73, 88, 122, 135–136
    disjoint —s, 29, 113

marking word for context, 89–91, 99
mass term, 133
masses, 122–124
mass-process, 4, 8, 12
Mates, Benson, 13
Mayan language, 28
McMurrin, Sterling M., 96
meaning, 13, 131–133
mind-body, 118

mistaken local categorematic word, 111
modifier(s), Chap 6 (17–20)
    redundancy of — 18
Moldovan, Dan, 132–133

names, 11
    replaced by description?, Chap 29 (119)
Navajo, 5, 133
"nearly", 20
negation,
    global, 38–39
    in mass-process languages, 134
    negative categorematic words and —, 42–44
    predicate — vs. propositional —, 134
negative categorematic words, Chap 10 (31–33)
    directing attention with —, 32
Nepali, 134
noncontradiction, principle of, 43
no-no, 42
non-, 31
non-non-, 32
null words, 33

objective claim, 124
objectivity, 124–125
open instance of a scheme, 100
overlapping contexts, 140–141

parentheses, 20
    not needed in disjoinings, 29
    not needed in together-uses, 22–23
part of the flow of all, 9
particular scheme of conceptual equivalences,
        61
paying attention
    concepts and —, 13
    directing attention with categorematic words,
        9, 35
    establishing context is directing attention, 10
    negative categorematic words and —, 32
    restricting ways of — in scenarios, 71
    See also context
PEGASUS, 11, 14, 19, 111, 112
Pelletier, F. J., 116
photograph for context, 70, 73
places, 136. See also location.
pointing, 34. See also context, establishing;
        paying attention.

Pokharel, Madhav, 134
possibility, 10
predicate logic, 11
predication, 22
premise(s), 66
   infinitely many?, 86
   schemes, 67
preposition, 28, 133
process-mass, processes. *See* mass-process.
processes vs. process, 4, 12, 21

quantity, 143
Quine, W.v.O., 11, 128

reasoning, system of,
   IXN, 80–81
   WMC, 107–108
   WMC+Local, 120
restricting contexts within general context, 74
Robinson, William S., 124
Rossetti, Christina, 24
rules for derivations,
   of conceptual equivalences, 61
   of words, 81
   of words marked for context, 108
   See also substitution.

same, 113–114
scenario, Chap 18 (69–72), 71
   hypothetical, 88
   with context words, 94–95
scheme(s),
   compatible instantiations of, 49–50, 100
   compound word —, 47
   initial — for conceptual equivalences, 61
   initial —for valid words, 79, 107–108
   instance of a —, 47, 100
      open —, 100
   instantiation(s) of —, 47
      compatible —, 49–50, 99–100
   of inferences, 67
      marked for context, 100
      marked for more than one context, 141–142
      marked for single context, 100
   of valid words, 80, 107–108
   of words, 47, 99–100
   of words marked for context, 100

scheme(s) (continued)
   open instantiation of —, 100
   valid — of words, 67, 105
   valid in scenario, 105
   word is an instantiation of some —, 49, 100
Schubert, L. K., 116
scientific law, 97
set-theory, 141
Sextus Empiricus 13
SIBLING, 58, 61, 63, 66, 78
single context, word scheme marked for, 100
solipsism, 13
space, 73
Strawson, Peter, 122, 135–136
subject of verb, 3
subjective claim, 124–125
subjectivity, inter—, 13, 125
substance, 10
substitution,
   of conceptual equivalences, 58
   of descriptive equivalences, 58
   rule of —, 60, 61, 72
syncategorematic word, 20
system of reasoning,
   IXN, 80–81
   WMC, 107–108
   WMC+Local, 120

Tatu, Marta, 132–133
therefore, 66
thing(s),
   derived from masses, 122–124, 135–136
   focus on just one —, 10–11
   individual —, 40, 136
      in talk of context?, 122
      names and —, 11
   persist in time through changes, 2, 119
   same —, 2, 113–114
   time-slice of a —, 11
   world made up of —, 3, 5
time, 73, 88, 124, 135–136
   context only specifies, 93, 115–117
time-slice of a thing, 11
together-uses of categorematic words,
   Chap 7 (21–25), 23
   order of words in— does not matter, 22–23
   physical inseparability and —, 21, 23
   redundancy in —, 23

Tough, Joan, 79
transitivity,
   of conceptual equivalence, 59, 61
   of deriving, 85
   of validity, 76
truth, 12

universal(s), 12, 15

valid inference, 66, 72
   derivable inference is valid, 84
   deriving —, Chap 20 (80–85)
   how to show —, 79
   in scenario, 71, 85
   reduced to validity of words, 78
valid word, 67, 72
   deriving —, Chap 20 (80–86), 81
   deriving valid compound words, 82
      in scenario, 85
   how to show word is valid, 79
      in scenario, 71

valid scheme of inferences, 67, 105
valid scheme of words, 67, 105
"very", 20

Waismann, Friedrich, 128–130
water, 116, 124
Wintu, 123, 133
WMC, 107–108
WMC+Local, 120
word,
   deriving in **IXN**, 80–81
   deriving in **WMC**, 107–108
   indexing — ?, 137–138
   is an instantiation of some scheme, 49
   marked for context, 89–91, 99
   See also categorematic word; compound
      word; valid word.
word scheme. *See* scheme, word.

There is no end, no beginning, but only the flow,
the becoming that is always becoming.
      from "She Who Loves the Lowest"
      in *The BARK of DOG*

www.ingramcontent.com/pod-product-compliance
Lightning Source LLC
Chambersburg PA
CBHW060932170426

43194CB00023B/2950